DISCARDED

Whither the Postmodern Library?

D1732767

DISCARDED

Whither the Postmodern Library?

Libraries, Technology, and Education in the Information Age

by

WILLIAM H. WISNER

McFarland & Company, Inc., Publishers
Jefferson, North Carolina and London

Front cover: *Juice* by William H. Wisner, 1999. Back cover: *Cancelled Cards* by William H. Wisner, 2000. Photos by Penelope Warren.

Library of Congress Cataloguing-in-Publication Data

Wisner, William H., 1956–
      Whither the postmodern library? : libraries, technology, and
education in the information age / by William H. Wisner
            p.   cm.
      Includes bibliographical references and index.
      ISBN 0-7864-0795-6 (softcover : 55# alkaline paper) ∞
      1. Academic libraries — Aims and objectives — United States.
      2. Libraries — United States — Special collections — Electronic
information resources.   I. Title.
      Z675.U5W76   2000
      027.7'0973 — dc21   00-35494

British Library cataloguing data are available

©2000 William H. Wisner. All rights reserved

*No part of this book may be reproduced or transmitted in any form
or by any means, electronic or mechanical, including photocopying
or recording, or by any information storage and retrieval system,
without permission in writing from the publisher.*

Manufactured in the United States of America

*McFarland & Company, Inc., Publishers
   Box 611, Jefferson, North Carolina 28640
   www.mcfarlandpub.com*

In memory of my father
Harold A. Wisner
whose library became the book of my heart
and for my daughters
Leah and Sophia
the grandchildren he never knew

SHATFORD LIBRARY

OCT   2000

PASADENA CITY COLLEGE
1570 E. COLORADO BLVD
PASADENA, CA 91106

Acknowledgments

I would like to express my thanks to my colleagues in the H. R. Yeary Library Reference Office for filling in for me while I was away on sabbatical leave in the spring of 1998 writing a good deal of this book. They include Len Cazares, Albert Bustos, Pedro Vasquez and Veronica Viera. I would also like to thank Teresa Dominguez, circulation supervisor, and her staff, for keeping things running smoothly in my absence.

I wish also to extend my gratitude to my professional colleagues at the Killam Library of Texas A&M International University in Laredo for reading parts of the manuscript and for making suggestions, particularly Mr. Rogelio Hinojosa and Dr. Gary Masters.

I am particularly grateful to the late Marvin Scilken — editor and publisher of *The Unabashed Librarian* — for publishing the original three-page article, "Whither the Postmodern Library?," which led to the present book. I also owe considerable moral support, both professionally and personally, to Dr. Paul Dubois, Former Director of the Dacus Library at Winthrop University in South Carolina.

Finally I wish to thank my wife Rosalba for managing things at home while I was engaged in the composition process and for encouragement, support and practical advice in the completion of this work.

William H. Wisner • *Laredo, Texas* • February 2000

Table of Contents

In this arrangement of values I may have gone astray at many points. It is up to others to try to do better. My one hope is that I have made the reader feel both the reality, difficulty and urgency of the problem and, at the same time, the scale and form which the solution cannot escape.

— Teilhard de Chardin,
The Phenomenon of Man

Preface

Maybe honesty is the best policy: I confess even after writing this little book to be still harboring significant levels of uncertainty about the future consequences of the collision between high technology and what I shall call educational values within the context of the new postmodern library.

It is more than uncertainty: it remains a species of confusion — a confusion all the more frustrating because I have been thinking about this issue obsessively for almost a decade. First as a librarian, with an obvious commitment to the profession; but also as a modestly educated man and passionate humanist; one who was graced by his parents and teachers with an unsentimental reverence for lifelong learning; and who recognizes, moreover, that the end of such learning is not self-fulfillment and happiness only, but the assumption of full citizenship within the greatest democratic experiment history has ever known.

On a personal level, I am convinced that Hannah Arendt is correct. "The end of learning," she has written, "is not knowledge but meaning."

On a social level, the fruits of a democracy cannot be sustained without an informed electorate that engages the pressing issues of its time and expresses its conclusions in the voting booth. Since libraries have always been one of the pillars of any structured education, their future is inseparable from true democratic learning, and we are correct to pose difficult questions about where libraries are headed and the role they will play in our collective future.

But perhaps uncertainty, at a time when history itself is undergoing profound changes with very long-term consequences, is an honorable thing to confess, never more than when we attempt to extrapolate that future out of the narrow slice of the present given us to ponder. Indeed, predictions about the future — especially when they are made by those most enthusiastic and utopian, like cybrarians today — have always turned out to be notoriously inaccurate, even on the scale of a few short decades.

When I was a young boy, dreamily turning over the leaves of my set of the Grolier *Book of Knowledge*, I read that by the year 2000 people would be lofting to work in speedy air cars, and trips to the moon — as a vacation getaway — would likely be common. In 1962 there would have been nothing glamorous about predicting the present we now live in, here at the turning millennium: increasingly neurotic individuals locked in metal boxes, commuting to work like faceless lemmings on clogged highways; spending as much as two hours a day driving to tedious jobs which will, if they are lucky, allow them just to meet the minimum payments on their credit cards.

Thus does conscience make cowards of us all, and our own enterprises of great pitch and moment — the globalization of information, the formation of a new world order based on unregulated capitalism wedded to democratic states, the steady progress of the biological sciences toward genetic engineering — may prove as illusory as once-predicted discount rates on Braniff flights to the Tycho crater.

That momentous technological change will be allowed by world events to continue uninterrupted is an expectation now so rooted in the mind of the common man — not to mention librarians themselves — that these expectations have by degrees been strangely reinscribed as actual duties to fulfill.

It is this unexamined and anti-historical conviction which has recently led librarianship down the primrose path of folly: the card catalog, to take but the most stellar example, was discarded by librarians overnight without a shred of discernible regret, remorse, seemliness or — most striking of all — consciousness of what such a sudden loss might mean either to the deep structures of the profession, their historical value or the impact of such a change on our users, especially older patrons, who are among the library's most loyal.

And, in fact, such short-sighted intellectual unawareness led directly to the embarrassing article hurled suddenly at us out of the blue in the hallowed pages (no less) of *The New Yorker* for April 4, 1994. Our glib profession has been in retreat from Nicholson Baker's seminal "Discards" ever since. When Baker's equally well-researched article on the book purges at the new San Francisco Public Library appeared, also in *The New Yorker*, in the October 14, 1996 issue — chronicling a series of decisions by then–Director Kenneth Dowlin positively sickening to read about and which led to his humiliating resignation — Baker, once a friend and lover of libraries, quickly became a pariah within librarianship: the corpse at the dinner party.

Baker won't go away, yet we hardly know what to say about this acclaimed, award-winning author's charges. So we have decided that ignoring Mr. Baker is the most expedient (though cowardly) course, even though there he is ... face down in the mashed potatoes.

Thanks to Mr. Baker's second *New Yorker* piece, a new term in the English language was profiled in the pages of the equally eminent *Atlantic Monthly's* "Wordplay" column: "guerrilla librarianship." It referred to attempts by certain of the librarians to "save" books at San Francisco Public by stamping them with erroneous due dates so that they would not be discarded under Mr. Dowlin's perverse reign of terror. Anyone who loves the sacred nature of learning, anyone reading Nicholson Baker's article about what actually went on at San Francisco Public, is justly disgusted by the priorities Mr. Dowlin set; just as they are right in condemning the too-timid "guerrilla librarians" for not doing nearly enough to stop the process.

In a profession which has always seemed to laymen to be driven by process over passion, by proscriptions and rules (*"shhhh!"*) instead of human warmth — and with a history made rich by denigrating stereotypes — Baker's southpaw punch has yet to be meaningfully addressed by broadly based discussion within the profession's leading journals. More damning still, no response written *by a librarian* has ever appeared in any of the major public journals where the attacks on our zealousness occurred.

And yet libraries — both the idealistic values which underlie them, and their larger role in the modern information revolution — have never been more on the minds of average persons than right at this very moment. This is due to the fabulous possibilities presented by CD-ROM, as well as the unprecedented public fascination generated by the Internet revolution.

The current popular passion for libraries — for incisive discussion of their possible future, for informed intellectual debate on the role of information in all our lives — is showing up in all the right magazines: *The New Yorker, The Atlantic, American Scholar, Daedalus*— and *Harper's,* which published a major feature in 1997 written by contributing editor Sally Tisdale and called "Silence Please." In this third, widely read and equally pejorative article about postmodern librarianship in a major magazine in less than three years, Ms. Tisdale took us to task for turning her beloved hometown library into an Alice's Restaurant of infotainment options: a library in which reverence had succumbed to relevance, an honorable atmosphere of quiet had declined into pure noise, and the hallowed experience of focused reading had been replaced by ubiquitous videoscreens and Net Nuts. Even the librarians she sought out for help couldn't for the life of them explain the classification system to her or help her find a book.

Obviously our best, most loyal users are trying very hard to tell us something: *A correction is needed.* Basic, core values are being deconstructed in front of our eyes; and librarians themselves are, through shallow boosterism, abetting this decline.

It is our patrons, frankly, who seem most concerned about where we are heading, not us. It is our patrons who keep bringing the discussion deftly back to the central question of human values, which are symbolized by the Book as the sacred, etymological foundation of librarianship. Our most thoughtful, earnest users are urging us to think deeply about and act circumspectly on the issue of technology — even as our *apparatchik* administrators are retooling budgets now wholly driven by the demands of pure, corporate, cynical, capitalist technology.

In my own community college library I watched a million-dollar automation system installed even while most of the book records I can now pull up onscreen, especially in the sciences and social sciences, are woefully out of date. The college's board of trustees, of course, credulously imagines that it has improved the condition of its taxpayers' library, and nobody in the administration itself is likely to discourage such a view.

And of course there is now little extra money remaining to buy books, in the social sciences or any other discipline. After spending so much on technology, you'd have to have the oratorical powers of Cicero to squeeze another dime out of the powers that be. It could hardly be maintained that this is a reality particular to our school.

For the first two years, using the DRA automated system we had bought — which we had been assured by company representatives (dressed in suits more expensive than I'll ever own, sporting truly *phenomenal* haircuts) was "state of the art" — I could not easily get a simple subject tracing onscreen to save my life. Instead of finding the tracing at the bottom of a paper card catalog card, visible at a glance, I had to issue two separate commands to get this major and routine piece of data. A student — even if he or she grasped the concept of subject tracings and how valuable they can be — would *never* have been able to intuit that they lay buried (in our "state of the art" system) behind an impenetrable "options" command.

Although recent migration to a web-based format has improved this aspect of our catalog, the fact remains that for two years — because we had, like everybody else, turned our paper card catalog into compost — student access to subject tracings was all but unheard of in our library; just as broad subject searches were a nightmare of trillions of subheadings, each requiring time-consuming separate commands to access, until one just gave up. This problem persists for us today and was never a feature of card catalogs, where "flipping and scanning" was easy.

It may very well be that the glut of books which began in the 1970s, and continues to the present day, forced the profession toward increasing computerization and doomed the card catalog out of sheer necessity. Keeping concurrent online and paper catalogs in huge university libraries comprising tens of millions of volumes surely would have been self-defeating and costly. But in midsize and smaller libraries I fail to see why concurrent catalogs could not have been maintained and could not still be maintained if they were made a priority — out of respect to "traditional" patrons uncomfortable with computers, and as a back-up to inevitable system crashes. Is such commonsensical prudence so outrageous to suggest?

Why have we put all our faith in a single, new, still-developing technology, and applied it across the board to libraries of every size, when a combination of solutions tailored and measured to specific needs might have been found to the benefit of everyone?

And this raises a central question: Even if *concurrent* catalogs were not kept, why in the name of God were the *old ones*, even if frozen, thrown away? What strain of bitter self-laceration prompted the destruction of a resource which for so long was the daily focus of thousands of catalogers, the record of decades of toil — the record also, and an irreplaceable one, of a great and mighty civilization.

Card catalogs represented by slow accretion the timely record of things which future scholars and historians might have found profoundly useful in ways no one can anticipate. But, incomprehensibly, we pulped it. Because we didn't love it. We didn't love the very thing we fashioned, at great cost, with great patience.

The card catalogs of all our libraries — certainly all the great libraries — should have been frozen and preserved, cared for as priceless artifacts which we, as librarians, felt duty bound to preserve. They could have been beautifully displayed; they could have been honored as part of our venerable past, like the *Book of Kells* or the First Folio. In their endearing wooden cabinets of oak and hardwoods and brass, they should have been given the reverence due them by time and sustained human intention and thought. As much as any book, they were the artifact of thought.

What is so appalling about discarding significant parts of the past so peremptorily — even with the best of intentions — is that the concept of "progress" by which such moves are always justified as imperatives may prove ephemeral considerations indeed in a disintegrating world. Though "progress" toward "globalization" of thought and information is best symbolized for librarians by the Internet (and, for economists, by the erasure of trade barriers), I see very little evidence that anything like real global thinking is going on, either inside or outside the library profession.

The planet appears — to this observer at least — to be hurtling out of control so fast under the twin pressures of overpopulation and environmental degradation that the survival of either Occidental or Oriental civilization is, I think, an entirely open question. We may very well find ourselves, in some epic global disaster, wishing for the card catalogs we trashed so thoughtlessly, when all telecommunication systems have been brought low.

Why librarians would be so unable to think "outside the box" on this I simply don't know. *We* were the ones who *saved* the classical world through the patient merits of preservation and copying during precisely the type of dark age I am talking about.

If anything, real global thinking would make us realize that we should, indeed, be acting "globally" out of pure, naked fear before the dreadful genies we have unwittingly conjured into being. Instead we spend our time restlessly combing through racks of jeans at the Gap, searching for authenticity. The Third World is falling to pieces at the same moment the First World is blithely pouring trillions of dollars into software and hardware.

Librarianship, though it may seem marginal to such an apocalyptic reckoning, has bought into the globalization paradigm with a vengeance — and is busy pouring its few billions into it. We will inherit the wind if we continue to do so, because we will have made information, not knowledge, let alone meaning, the center of what we do. At that fateful moment, the mechanical will have replaced the humane.

The consequences of this chichi trendspotting have the power to destroy the humanistic roots of the profession or bend it out of recognizable shape forever. Indeed I believe the process of devaluation in our profession, as in the larger world to which we are linked, is already very far advanced. Because I do value silence, reverence, and deep reading, I wonder what will happen to libraries and librarians unless we examine the true, traditional nature of our intentions and what concrete priorities they dictate for us. A profession which has heroically saved civilization once — in the intense, inward silence of the Medieval scriptoria — should not beggar its own history by contributing to the unexamined disintegration of culture going on everywhere we look, from the cradle to the mall.

Individual men and women, the professions they create, and nation-states themselves succeed or fail by acknowledging that human values can indeed be determined, followed, defended and promoted. Ethics — integrity — cannot be divided from the personal, professional or political domains. It cannot be divided from education. It must not be divided from librarianship, which plays a role of service — both eminently practical and ethical — in the life of any true civilization. And librarians should not actively serve any system which manifestly prioritizes mere information over knowledge, introduces and then worships change as a serious end in itself, helps dethrone the sacred Book from the center of our educational lives and substitutes in its place an addictive online experience.

We have spent a decade grooming a reference area based on speed, self-direction, non-human scale and "efficiency." Our reward has been to increasingly de-center the librarian from his patrons — who have rightly concluded that (except perhaps to change the printer paper) he is no longer really needed.

If technology is, indeed, a "mere" tool, then why is it being allowed to run us ragged in endless collection development committee meetings, exploding our budgets for traditional materials, and turning us and the staff into frazzled wrecks with new programs, new graphical interfaces, and a steady stream of new upgrades you can be certain Bill Gates and his kind have ensured *will never end?*

Is suggesting prudence and moderation and the slow, carefully managed — and therefore fiscally sustainable and seemly — introduction of information technology really so outrageous? Why, then, do I see no evidence of such a balanced, prudent and skeptical attitude? Why are 90 percent of the articles I read in *Library Journal* written by blandly utopianistic lemmings hurtling off cliffs? How will "information globalization" be made truly useful and resonant and humanly meaningful by a generation of librarians so ignorant of the traditional values and heroism cemented into their own history?

Anything worthily human and humane requires patience, time,

prudence and moral courage to set in place. The real values which formed librarianship were not achieved in so-called real time, or by simply pressing <enter>. Librarians have, quite simply, lost their dignity as well as their common sense in a shameless pursuit of technology — and Nicholson Baker and Sally Tisdale merely pointed that out to us at our own little dinner party.

The present book, though justifiably uncertain about the long-term future of libraries given the rapidity of change now engulfing us, is *not* confused about the honorable past which lies behind us. We have quietly stood for certain ineffable values which I will undertake to outline more specifically in the following pages. The seductive new information technologies — so useful, so powerful, so rightfully awesome if rightly used — are nevertheless currently subverting both libraries and librarians.

I am certain librarians are abandoning the *logos* for the LAN without a single backward glance. The warnings of our more prescient fellows are lingering in the air behind us, as we play out a ritual action as seemingly fated and inevitable as a tragedy by Aeschylus.

I hope, through examples and commentary drawn from my own personal, professional and educational life, to examine here what is being lost or is already gone; to range widely beyond libraries to look both at the present context of education and the current state of the world; and especially to make it clear that those of us within the profession who are signaling the need for prudence will never yield to the lie that what we oppose is technology per se, the potential for science to better us in entirely unexpected ways, or the ability of technology to enhance the experience of human meaning in the new age that surely is to come.

Chapter 1

The Winter of Knowledge

I met him in 1985, in my first year of library school. We never knew each other well — and indeed Dr. Spencer Shaw almost certainly has forgotten my name, although today he would, I think, recognize me as a friend; someone whom he passed daily in the vaulted, Gothic hallways of grand old Suzzallo Library on the University of Washington campus, where he taught children's librarianship. His kindly face and dignified bearing crept slowly into my awareness. I began to admire him, from a distance. True learning is always a collection of such alchemies — stray influences which can later blossom into a broad life view. One teaches, as Shaw did, and one implicitly stands for something; and if one embodies an ideal, the young of any age will know it and respond.

This aging, silver-haired black professor extolled the value of children's literature by giving incomparable readings to young people of all ages at libraries throughout the Puget Sound region, sacrificing his Saturday mornings in the service of reading and books after a tiring week of classes. It was at the Graduate School of Library and Information Science at Washington where I first learned that people who use libraries as children have been found to use them consistently as adults; that the early connection to the transcendent word follows one throughout one's life. It has been so in my own.

I write from the border of things, far removed now from the border of Washington state, here at the other edge of America, in Laredo, Texas. If reading is to be vindicated it must be vindicated here, where our bilingual Hispanic population searches restlessly for a way into the American dream. Interstate 35 begins at International Bridge No. 1 downtown and does not rest till Canada. The best students at the community college library (where I have worked as a reference librarian for a decade) are eager to learn and have much to overcome. Still embarrassed to be called "Mr. Wisner" and "Sir," when I was a student myself for so long, I realize that I represent something essential for the students as I log my hours at the reference desk each day, answering questions of every kind.

"Mr. Wisner, where is the Ivory Coast?"

"Sir, I need a metric conversion table."

"Do you have the book *The Immense Journey*?"

I am aware, especially with older, nontraditional students, what a broad, decisive line they're crossing just to put these questions to me — stepping beyond the borders of one culture to confess a need and inquire information from a fair-haired gringo in a white shirt and tie. In a growing city remarkable still for its ethnic narrowness — and saturated with all the formality and respect for learning which inhere in Hispanic culture — I turn out to be something of an important commodity. If I can claim anything for myself, it is that I am privileged now to stand unsentimentally for the books which invented me, before a populace whose only road into the future — intellectual and practical — is through the written word. The guiding example of Spencer Shaw, in short, has been transmuted across race, space and time into a new and profound reality.

In the past decade, libraries underwent two separate revolutions. The first revolution came, as every librarian knows, in the form of CD-ROM; and I watched it reshape public services in our library almost overnight. In less than a year, CD-ROM opened a new era in information retrieval, often making my job easier and positively delighting students, who made fruitful use of the new searching capabilities they permit. Old paper indexes like *The Readers' Guide* or *Education Index* became, in the blink of an eye, a race of overwrought, winded dinosaurs, tottering on their limbs — not quite dead yet but getting there. Like my colleagues across the country, I now watch bemused as students wait in a line for 20 or 30 minutes to use a computerized index (and its obliging printer) while perfectly useful paper indexes lie already vanquished and unused — stupendously banged into obscurity with the same giddy renunciation an important new technology always produces. Whatever one's reservations about mushrooming technological advances, CD-ROM bore witness to the birth of a new consolidation in the written word — the digitization of print into infinitely manipulable bytes of data.

The second revolution in Yeary Library occurred more recently, with the introduction of the Internet. Popular as CD-ROM had been, it is possible that CD-ROM itself — and against all expectation, considering how it was ballyhooed by the information utopianists — has itself become a kind of dopey ichthyosaur in exactly the same way paper indexes did. Everything is migrating rapidly to the Net, thus bypassing CD-ROM, with the identical enhanced search capabilities the beguiling rainbow disks provide. Future refinements to the Internet, such as conventional subject cataloging, can be expected to make finding information on the World Wide Web even easier than it already is.

The advent of the Internet in our library inaugurated a new and unprecedented era of student use. For the first time, students are appearing in impatient pods when I open the building at 7:30 each morning. We have to forcibly evict them at closing time. In the period between, the Internet terminals our library now provides are in constant use, as are the two behemoth printers unrolling their endless pages. How wonderful, we all thought at first. Finally, something exciting in the library!

But my colleagues and I soon discovered that it was not a passion for Chaucer, geometry or Texas history which was roping students into the building. It was, instead — perhaps inevitably — their passion for chatlines, web pages featuring either Brad Pitt or supermodels, the use of e-mail to communicate with friends met at Padre Island during spring break, or — in the case of a few bold students, both men and women — pure, hardcore porn.

The students at our school, like students everywhere, have already vindicated these startling new technologies with unprecedented glee. As in so many dimensions of American life, the god of Information has been elevated to such an eminence that library science has had to follow suit, sensing, with the same giddy enthusiasm, a source of rebirth for a discipline long occupying one of the lower rungs of the academic ladder.

Meetings are being held. Memos fly hot between departments. Budgets are being feverishly retooled to purchase the new, expensive information altars, which every library now must have. Of course it is not only students who are demanding such services. With few exceptions (such as increasingly beleaguered English professors over age 60) faculty members also require "access" at every level which their institutions can decently finance to further research and publication. Technology is more than utility. More even than convenience. For libraries, technology is status.

The winds of a new *zeitgeist* are blowing north by northwest. Every day, I read dutifully through the professional literature in my discipline. Glossy notices announcing the birth of new databases litter my desk by the dozens. In letters promoting such services I am now addressed as "Dear Information Specialist," rarely as "Dear Librarian." We must admit that such technologies — by general agreement — now represent the future of librarianship at every level of service and as a separate degreed program in accredited institutions. Surely only kooks or recalcitrants would resist such a change, modern day Luddites of the fringe.

As so much potential throbs before me; as I watch the computers with their unsleeping cobalt screens pulsing without effort or fatigue not six feet away from "my" reference desk; as I face down the future with an even stare and confront what it is I meant by my life, I feel a chill modern alienation creeping into my frame, as if I'm trapped in a play by Ionesco. I have been in librarianship for over ten years. Elder today, a session wiser, and fainter too, as wiseness is, I find myself still softly searching ... for my delinquent palaces.

The woman who wrote that last sentence — the poet Emily Dickinson — was a reader all her life. She had the habit of books, living with them in isolation in her father's imposing mansion in Amherst. She would not have considered herself remarkable in that love of written things, with the beloved gold letters stamped upon the worn calf bindings in her father Edward Dickinson's library. Picked up, set down, in the grief that was her life, books became Emily Dickinson's friends — spots of joy in the reclusive boundaries she opted for, in writing a letter to the world that never wrote to her.

24

Education and life-long learning — in which libraries can play so large a role — are as delicate in their own way as this spinster poet ever was. As information becomes knowledge and (in the encounter with one's personal self) knowledge becomes meaning; as the budding heart blooms into awareness, the values it embraced at the beginning of its pilgrimage may also be transformed. Rarely will truth turn out to be what one was told it must be, whether by one's teachers, friends, colleagues or lovers. Rarely if ever will it reflect a trend — like the current Information mania, or the unduplicatable lives of Hollywood celebrities, or the new avocado diet plan.

The state of mind this book is aiming at is entirely inward. It can be murdered by many things: by the negative values of overweening pride, the desire for great wealth, youthful passion that is converted into mere careerism. And — especially for young and inexperienced minds (precisely those most vulnerable and therefore precious) — it can be hamstrung and ruined by an idolatry for mere Information, as our society has digitized it, computerized it, homogenized it and commodified it.

Rightly used and rightly comprehended, information technology can be a great blessing and an incredible timesaving tool. But such technology is neither a necessary, nor even a sufficient, condition to guarantee knowledge and the reverence for truth out of which human meaning and the highest human values may grow. Information technology (and we all know exactly what that means, from the Internet to an unthinkable Virtual Reality just around the corner) is promiscuous, prurient, addictive. It can provide an escape from reality, but that escape is *not* the equal of the good, imaginative escape one can find between the covers of a book.

Loving the life of the mind with all of one's heart and soul, and then wedding it to the experience of living: These are the only absolutely necessary conditions for enlightenment. If one worships Information as an end in itself — which is one of the principal values librarianship is now actively helping to promote — one has gone wrong at the first turn as surely as if one had succumbed to an enervating addiction of any kind. The notion that a student *must* have access to technology, or computerized card catalogs, or FirstSearch databases in order to become educated is a dismal, false lie in an increasingly valueless and meaningless world. Promoting such a pernicious belief at a time when a shocking number of students in America do not have the habit of reading or cannot write a competent paragraph, let alone a term paper, is well nigh criminal.

Librarianship is active, not passive; it has a direct positive obligation to reflect its core values in the person of the librarian, who alone humanizes the library. If the librarian has bought into the information game heart and soul, the students he or she can transform through example will ultimately be diminished. Sooner or later a machine will replace the librarian — and rightly so. A machine can help students, but it cannot love them.

I believe librarianship's sense of its core values — its human and educational values — is in precipitous decline. We must then ask what values have graced our profession's history thus far? The first and foremost has been fittingly stated: to love the truth and to seek it through education. Also, to promote the achievement of literacy and of reading as inherently affirmative, proper to the only creature in this part of the cosmos endowed with reason — a creature able to reflect on itself, and on its terrible aloneness; a creature which can also seek, and find, a rational and plausible future.

It follows that the sum of the best of human thought is represented in democracy, whose responsibilities are twofold: the fullest development of one's happiness through lifelong commitment to the truth and virtuous action; and the maintenance of the republic through informed political choice. In this, libraries — both public and academic — play a direct and time-honored role. It has not always been so: with Hypatia's murder at Alexandria we lost; in the book-burnings of Nazi Germany we lost; in censorship of any kind, libraries, librarians — and the larger society — always lose.

Sometimes such losses are reversible, minor. But at other times whole world orders may be threatened. Remember Iona, the sceptered isle at the edge of nothingness, at the bath of the forbidding North Atlantic, at the edge of the disintegrating Roman Empire, but which yet enjoyed a moment of glory, which yet reclaimed — through the painstaking toil of monks in its medieval *scriptoria*— what few fragments of the ancient world were to come down to us; not there only, but at monasteries across Ireland, and at isolated monastic outposts throughout Europe as barbarity and ignorance engulfed the Empire and the darkest age the West has ever known put out its claw to silence all that was best in us.

The scholar-librarians in their holy orders — at times uncertain even of the meaning of the text set before them to copy — quite literally saved Western civilization; eventually transmitted what could be found and preserved to the learning centers and libraries of the budding Renaissance; and from that reclamation of the ancient world set humanity, both East and West, on the road to a future only now achieving fruition: the rise of science and democracy out of the Enlightenment, each unthinkable without the other, always and necessarily growing in tandem with each other, the golden braid of modern thought.

Anonymity, not glory; conviction before weariness; strength before barbarity; a sense of the sacred *logos*, which informs the mind despite its eternal and unsleeping doubts: This *was* our history.

A dozen corollaries for librarianship follow from such reverence: tolerance for new ways of thinking and new ideas; the promotion of education and scholarship by example, in the generalist's love of learning which every librarian must strive to embody; the ability also of librarianship as a profession to sort and teach priorities of knowing into hierarchies of importance (information — without context and yet absolutely necessary — being merely the basement level of a higher knowledge at which the upward-driving mind must aim); a horror before plagiarism and borrowed thinking, or censorship of any kind, as immoral within the constraints of the scholarly life; veneration of the West's tradition, which is increasingly the world's, but which yet must be questioned and tested anew with each human generation; the conviction, finally, that — beginning with the *logos*— the human journey toward its promised end lies in a progression from information to knowledge, and thence to meaning, and finally to wisdom, which contemplates its own mortality and all that it might mean.

All these ineffable values the Book implies. It is our sacred symbol. Not for nothing does "library" come from the Latin, "liber." Librarians, now more than ever, must speak for the book, stand for the book, not preside over its dreadful termination in an unfeeling plastic disk.

The master's degree in library science is not a true "subject" degree and can still be earned at many accredited library schools in a single year. Despite vigorous, and even quaintly endearing, attempts to gain credibility by appearing "theoretical" or "scientific," library education has really always been emphatically practical and service-oriented —

and indeed to master the concepts of indexing and cataloging and learn about major reference sources and the psychological dynamics of what is called the "reference interview" requires no great intellectual effort beyond enthusiasm and energy. One learns mostly by doing, and one learns it on the job. There is nothing to apologize for in this. We are not a "deep" profession. We are an idealistic one.

In librarianship, as in few other modern disciplines in the academy, idealism is triumphant, unapologetic and naïve. In the increasingly overspecialized university, in which even the humanities have too often been professionalized into cynical "critical theories," the generalist librarian can witness to the singleness of *veritas*, its perspicacious unity in variety and its ultimate indivisibility. Such witness, in an era of general diminishment in American education, is a noble role to play *if* one's values are durable and well tested—*if*, in short, one's heart and mind are liberally educated.

I believe the elevation of information over knowledge in librarianship has coincided with a general loss of ethical vision across the board in American education—a widely discussed pattern we have seen especially in philosophy (whose professionalization in the university undermined truth) and English studies (whose professionalization undermined meaning). Librarianship shares in this decline. The journal literature authored by librarians, which I must honestly force myself to read, is so abysmally written one can tell most of it was cobbled together by people who apparently have no feel for the beauty and glory of English prose. Acronyms surface without embarrassment like bobbing ducks (ASCII, OCLC, NOTIS, NITWITNET), and computer jargon dominates a style which is actually antithetical to the habit of true learning. In the articles I read, for example, students are "end-users" and books are "information resources," or, in one recent memorable example, "information objects"! Knowledge, as the ground and context in which mere information must be placed, is rarely extolled as the sinew that binds the profession together except by sporadic lip service. Not surprisingly, as the American Library Association and other professional organizations urge librarians to become "pro-active" and "gatekeepers" of the new information deities, the articles librarians write for each other focus increasingly on the forms, intentions and language of business and the values of marketing. Not scholarship. Not even books. But "access."

Since 1978, over a dozen schools of librarianship have closed across the country, including — unbelievably — the Graduate School of Library Science at Columbia University: the nation's oldest graduate library school, founded by Melvil Dewey himself in 1887. The nation's second most esteemed library school, at the University of Chicago, has also closed its doors. Lightning bolts of debate flashed hot in the journals when the closings were at their height, asking how such diminishments — in the Information Age, moreover! — are to be understood.

It has been noted, by those both in and outside the field, that library schools are currently having extreme difficulty in defining what specifically it is that they do — specifically, what values comprise the core of the profession to distinguish it from related fields like records management, communications or the computer sciences. Such an uncertainty over priorities — which can be healthy in times of rapid, even revolutionary change — needs resolution. It is here that the correction I am urging us to make — away from our relentless recent focus on technology and back toward humane values — must come. Redefining librarianship under the aegis not of knowledge, but of information technology, will, I am convinced, assure our end and give away what was best in us.

In the long run, I think librarians will be used by the information god and then discarded, because of the increasing privatization of information. Commercial vendors and suppliers of information will display a short memory for the gullible "information specialists" they have been courting and testing their products on before making a strenuous, calculated move into the private sector. Indeed, such a capitalist program, driven by a bottomless market of well-primed consumers, is already well underway. Enhancements, endless updates, gaudy gizmos and extra, needless and expensive buttons to push will assure AOL, Compuserve and other service providers not yet in existence steady profits into the foreseeable future; all the high-priced, empty-headed paraphernalia America markets better than anyone else. For librarianship to gullibly follow the lead of such disingenuous corporate sponsors will surely doom whatever remains of the profession's honor.

History justly teaches us that even noble traditions can be lost in a single flagrant generation. We librarians are managing to trade our only tradition for no tradition. When the last university administrator firmly and finally merges the last library school into the computer

29

science department, the sad, glorious legacy of Iona — calling plaintively to us across the centuries — will, at last, be truly dead. Too late will we realize that library science, in its own shy way, was always and properly a part of the humanities — which fixes its eyes on eternal things — and that it destroyed itself by trying to become a second-rate science.

It is almost an afterthought that modern-day librarians have tragically misplaced the heritage they helped to invent and, in the process, further impoverished education in our time. Our profession is not alone in losing its bearings, as we shall see in a subsequent chapter. And, sadly, reference librarians were the last licensed generalists left in academe to speak for that heritage. Ultimately, of course, it is the future which will pay — the students we are pledged to serve, like the ones I work with every day; students who often seem surprised and uneasy that the computerized quick-fixes they are now used to, and which I have provided, can do little to help them write a solid, well-argued research paper on *Paradise Lost* and its deep examination of pride.

Now more than ever, academic librarians must see their students in their present diminishment and recognize their severe limitations in an age when competing claims — from MTV and Tommy Hilfiger to the timeless burden of parental expectations — make life for young men and women extraordinarily complex and troubled. Their turmoil and longing, so palpably visible in the wake of the freshly disintegrated nuclear family, and their nobility — to be in a classroom, any classroom, in a world positively hostile to the idealism youth both requires and deserves — is the foundation of my love for them. *What love can do, then let love attempt*, Romeo says to his beloved in Shakespeare's play about youthful purity. And I will help them — I mean I will help Roxanne and Murti and Clarissa and Mr. Robles and Mr. Benavides and the countless other good men and women, young and old, I have known, whether they are laboring over a book or a periodical or attempting to provoke education to meaning in front of a computer screen. In this world, one could do worse, much worse. We are always at the border of untruth, feeling for the known, just as I am now at the very limit of the West.

Generating information is easy — a mere stopover in the basement of what one of my classics professors movingly called "the several storied tower of learning." In a time when librarians have been widely granted faculty status by their institutions, it is incumbent on us to eschew the trivial, see "information" for the deceptive temptation it is, and admit that the rigors of actual learning cannot be side-stepped; that knowledge is and always was a patient, sometimes wearying process in which memory and enthusiasm must combine to produce understanding. *The only educators who matter now must embody an ethical component in academic life which students manifestly long for and rarely receive.*

Some years ago, on a return visit to Seattle, I ran into Spencer Shaw, who was waiting for a bus on the University of Washington main drag. I was aware that he had retired since I last saw him. Although a scholarship had been established in his name there at the school, I learned that his position in children's librarianship (one of two) had not been renewed. Instead a young, publishing expert in relational databases had been given his post. It was one of those little upsets, so common in academe, in which current values are articulated.

Professor Shaw seemed surprised when I greeted him by name and shook his hand in what I know now was a farewell. I looked back once, briefly, and then not again. He stood waiting for the bus, without a companion in the littered street, amidst the punkers, panhandlers and skinheads. For a moment I was actually afraid for him. It was chilly, winter in Seattle. I remember his coat collar was turned up as he got on the bus.

Perhaps it *is* true, I thought, that libraries are about silence most of all; and, in some impossible way, about the care I suddenly felt for Spencer Shaw and the dignity and great privilege of his life. And that the diminishment of libraries, moreover, has always signaled a disquieting decline in civilization.

Chapter 2

Good Technology, Bad Technology

A story about technology, which I must tell at length.

My father, in the last year of his life, had grown increasingly despondent. Cancer had exacted its usual high toll on his resilience, physically and mentally. But I viewed with sharp concern another development in his decline which — living as I did, so far away — I felt almost powerless to halt. I came to realize, on a solitary trip to Seattle, that physical, emotional and psychological decline were not the chief diminishments drawing him further and further into pessimism. A malignant spiritual malaise had come over him which, as a retired Presbyterian minister, must have greatly troubled him and his entire view of his past. And it was during this visit, after I had flown up to the Pacific Northwest from Laredo, full of good news about marriage and work, that I perceived — for the first time — that his smiles and affirmations were being rendered more by duty than by conviction. He was putting on a good show.

As a man of God, who had comforted countless parishioners with pastoral reassurances, how could he tell me the awful suspicion which I alone believed began to overwhelm him: that God — his, ours, the once-believed-in center he had spoken for, stood for, and in whose name he had consigned people to the grave — was silent?

My father's library, of course, was some comfort to him, as was his Mozart — especially *The Magic Flute,* his favorite opera. Despite incessant pain from the cancer which made him grimace occasionally as we would talk — each tightened line on his face causing me grief, for I had never had to endure what he was going through, minute after minute — it was, I think now, the silence his family was locking him into which galled me the most. My three older brothers, all physicians and surgeons, had charted every aspect of his care and overseen it competently and efficiently; and my mother and he had grown demonstrably closer as the inevitable approached. Indeed they seemed to enjoy a happiness almost nonexistent as I was growing up, and I was gratified to see this undeniable fact. Yet none of them knew him as I knew him: as a writer, poet and artist I alone grasped his vulnerable poetic heart and the reach of the literary sensibilities which he would inevitably be using to "decode" what was happening to him.

One day he called me over next to the great window looking out onto the green yard filled with huge pink and white rhododendrons and velvety mosses which he had tended so lovingly up until about a year ago.

"You don't like librarianship much, do you?" he asked.

"No," I replied, truthfully, since I perceived that he wanted the truth from me and that I, too, had been engaging in a similarly complex lie with the rest of the family.

"Do you think you ever could? It's a worthy enough thing, Bill."

"Only if I can write about it," I replied, "Only if librarianship can somehow be restored to the humanities again, where it belongs. Barbara would have wanted me to at least write about that, I think."

"You miss her?"

"I don't think about her, Father. I never really grieved, you know. Anger's more like it. But she was probably the best librarian the Corcoran ever had. After she died the reason for our having the same degree — even the same profession — died with her. I'm not complaining, by the way. Rosalba and I have a good life, a fine life. We want kids. I like what I'm doing enough to stay with it for awhile. I can't say much more than that, I guess. And to love books — first and only that — that was sort of the point of the whole thing you and Mom taught me."

He motioned me closer with his broad, scarred hand. A childhood accident with his mother's stove had so scarred his palms that no palm-lines remained.

"We're all skaters on a lake, Bill," he said sadly, his voice and his spirit already very far away. "A lake ringed by mountains. And we all know the ice is melting from underneath."

Suddenly, for the first and only time in my life, I was a little afraid of him.

We had always shared a secret that my brothers, being scientists, had never shared with him: a reigning passion for interpreting things that lay at the very crux of our souls. He and I — and I think this is the truth — shared some necessary and inexplicable need to always feel "in meaning"; a need almost wholly foreign to most people whom I know. If our meaning departs, we die. Whether the text was the Bible or *King Lear* did not matter. It was that the characters peopling these works — their motivations, surrenders and triumphs — were more real and necessary to the maintenance of our inner lives than we could possibly explain to others, or perhaps admit to ourselves.

For example, it was because my father had studied the Jesuit scientist Pierre Teilhard de Chardin, that I felt compelled to read the dissident theologian's *Phenomenon of Man* when I was 12. It was not only that I learned something about evolution and anthropology from reading Teilhard, which was the point, even though I had set myself the formidable task of comprehending him at too young an age. No, I also read Teilhard because my father loved him, and handled his books respectfully as I watched, awestruck, in the church library there on Howard Street. In our home, books vindicated life. They would be the route to immortality if one of us was ever to write one. No one ever realized I, the last born, had silently vowed to do so.

His comment, then, about the skaters on the lake — about the absurdity of life, the inevitability of death, the delusions and conventions which social man always adopts to make erasure bearable — was thus a direct challenge to me. Sitting in the chair by the fire, I searched my mind wildly for a way to reassure him even as death was clawing him from me, those freezing fingers were even now stroking his gentle, crucified face. That my father did not complain nor behave with unmanly self-pity was all the more galling. I knew he was going to go down without saying what was in his heart to the rest of them. I knew this was my last chance.

I chose my words carefully, throttling my own enormous doubts.

"You remember that story about Mahler?" I said offhandedly. "They hated the Second Symphony. His best friend, an eminent music critic, said, 'This is not music.' That one comment shut him down for five years. Then he wrote the conclusion, you know."

"In the mountains," my father replied.

"That's right. Alma would bribe the shepherd boys not to let the clinking of the sheep's bells disturb him."

"Must've been something for him. The Swiss mountains, wasn't it? He must've felt free," my father said, brightening a little.

"Let me put on the final movement. Remember the subtitle of the symphony, Dad?" I asked casually. *I was going to force him to say it.*

"Resurrection Symphony."

Our stereo was, along with the wall of books in his hand-crafted library, my father's dearest possession. Whenever I came home he never failed to remind me, with an almost bumpkin Midwestern pride, that each speaker had cost "over a thousand dollars," and that my mother had hotly protested such extravagance, and was still doing so.

The chords of the final movement of *Resurrection Symphony* broke the stillness and gloom of the house, the lowering Seattle light and incessant rain, which seemed to symbolize the baleful sadness of my father's infirmity. Yet within the musical canon no work could have been more suited to the purpose I was intending: to restore, as a matter of love and duty, some element of hope to my father; to somehow pierce and banish, if only for a moment, the gloom which had descended upon his heart, and refute the spiritual malaise which had metastasized throughout his faith. I turned up the volume in the empty house.

Mahler's youthful masterpiece paints a picture in sound of the ending of the world. The first half of the long movement evokes, with terrifying sonic upheaval, the sundering of the earth and the opening of graves as piercing, discordant trumpets announce the Apocalypse. The first half of the movement is loud, fearful, discordant and shrill—

and tinged with the terror of summons, which Modernism in music is perfectly equipped to convey.

The dissonance and fear of the first part of the fifth movement, however, gives way, in the second part, to the soft entrance of the chorus and its soaring soprano. The text begins after a trembling silence and brooding, then builds with monumental strength.

> You will rise again, yes, rise again
> My mortal dust, after a short repose....
>
> All that you lived for is yours, yes, yours;
> All that you loved and fought for....
>
> Oh believe: *you did not live and suffer in vain....*

At this point in the music I silently shifted my chair closer to my 74-year-old father as he listened with eyes closed and head bent to the music, which a young man, in a former century, had written from great mountains ringing frozen lakes.

What was my father feeling for, prayerfully, as he sat there concentrating? For it *was* a kind of prayer. I had seen him pray, in better days, when certainty still sat upon his shoulder. The same rapt, intense concentration. Was he feeling the growing presence of some absolute ending, drawing strength from Mahler's music to meet the lean, abhorred demon straight on? Was he grieving, perhaps, for me, his youngest son, for my ruined youth that plucked one fiancée from me without even a chance to say good-bye? Or his own marriage which had faltered, and made his middle years ambivalent as he summoned the necessary strength to ascend a pulpit every Sunday to address a multitude destined never to comprehend, as in every age?

I think, and here memory almost fails me. I think he was remembering the green yard outside the picture window, the yard he once tended so proudly, the yard so like the original Garden lying somewhere in all our mythic past; and then maybe out to the forested islands of Puget Sound, set in the cold waters of the porpoise, where, in 1987, my eldest brother Byron had flung the ashes of his wife, dead from leukemia. I think he was remembering the Sound receding forever into the line of the peninsular Olympics on a farther shore. I think — I can only hope — that he and Mahler were, at that moment, one united personality. And that art (which lies beyond and above religion and its dogmas) was feeding its electric power into his shifting, ramifying soul.

As we listened, the voices built to an unbearable climax, and the orchestra and the choir suddenly sheared apart, sundered in a reign of brass. Against all expectation, it was the orchestra that entered into Mahler's version of the infinite, as the chorus stayed behind. I reached over, then — a great pain bursting in my heart — and took his scarred hand in mine. The grip which came back was not the grip of death, but that of a man of strength, courage and dignity. We sat there, we two, neither of us sad, for once. Time — banished and puny — no longer mattered.

Several months later I received the inevitable call from my brother David, on a Sunday, while stationed at the reference desk. We had just opened for the day.

"Bill," David said brokenly, "our dad passed away three minutes ago, at home. Steve and I were holding him. Now I think you should...," and then he choked off into quiet sobs.

"Are you aware, David," I said with a slow dawning, "that he died at ten o'clock your time — the same hour he always delivered his sermon?" A few moments later, I spoke again. "Look, Rosie and I will be there tomorrow. And thank you for being with him, for all that you and Steve have done."

Typically at such moments, I had no tears. Those would come later, and for many years following. Death, farewell, and art are interlaced lovingly in my strange, hybrid soul. I felt relief in the ending of his pain, and a manly certainty in the integrity of his life on earth. My dialogue with books began with him, in his library. I informed the staff of the news and phoned for a replacement. Then I called my wife.

My brothers and mother asked me to assemble a memorial service for my father — despite the short notice and the intervening distance — since they felt, I suppose, that I knew his inner life, at least from a poetic point of view, better than anyone else. Readings were to be the core of the service, with participation by any family member wishing to do so. In the interval before our plane lifted off from the Laredo International Airport I jotted down ideas for the service, then called a local friend and fellow-librarian, John Hastings, for some assistance with an idea I had.

With me on the plane I also took a single book: my father's copy of *Report to Greco* by Nikos Kazantzakis, the Greek author who first gained worldwide fame with his novel *Zorba the Greek. Report to Greco,* published posthumously, is Nikos's moving spiritual autobiography whose reigning personal presence is the painter El Greco, the artist from Crete, Kazantzakis's homeland. El Greco's magnificent painting *Toledo in the Storm* becomes for the author the symbol of Crete's molten passion, violence, and rude, stubborn vindication of life's bitter, undying beauty.

Kazantzakis was an author introduced to our family by my brother David's wife, Tricia, and her father, the late psychiatrist Owen Otto. He was, along with Teilhard de Chardin, Miguel de Unamuno, Shusako Endo, Paul Tillich, Dietrich Bonhoeffer, Jacques Maritain and Martin Buber one of a handful of thinkers who influenced my father's thinking about faith most profoundly. No doubt heretically.

Moreover, this copy of *Report,* which my father had given to me when I came to Laredo in 1988, was very special: a Faber edition with a light reddish-orange cover featuring a portrait of El Greco. My father had purchased this copy, published in London, in a bookseller's stall in Athens within sight of the Acropolis, when our family visited Greece in the mid–1970s. Two days later we had boarded a cramped, all-night steamer with blaring *bouzouki* music and made the passage to Crete. By then my father had already begun making notes on the book, writing them down on thin leaves of cobalt-blue airmail paper. I still keep these notes in the book.

Whenever I handle my father's copy of *Report to Greco* now, the memory of Crete and its freshening, sun-washed air come back to me — and that lemon and almond-scented afternoon in January 1977 when we visited Kazantzakis's grave outside Heraklion. I was 21 years old. The site, up a white graveled road, is not far from the fascinating excavations of ancient Knossos. The inscription on Nikos's simple gravestone likewise recurs to me:

I hope for nothing.
I am afraid of nothing.
I am free.

A rude, wooden cross made of timbers is set into the rough granite of the gravesite next to the smooth rectangular block of limestone on which the author's epitaph is carved. Beyond it, on the horizon, a line of mountains lifts into the sky. Beyond the mountains, invisible but certain, is Homer's very own wine dark sea.

My wife and I arrived, exhausted, in Seattle by day's end, and were soon in Bellingham, near the Canadian border, where two of my brothers live. Byron, my eldest brother, had also flown in from Montana. It was the first time since my marriage that the entire family had been assembled in one place.

The next day we all gathered on the back patio of David's mountainside property, where seats had been arranged beneath the tall conifers of the northern forest. The April air was cool. Fogs had drifted past in the morning, but a light shower had cleared the air, leaving everything dew-laden and scented. The small cassette player I had requested from David sat on a table next to a large overhanging apple tree, white with blossoms, which clung to the mossy stones of an embankment.

"You all know," I began, "that our father, Harold Wisner, loved the works of Kazantzakis, which he had learned about through Tricia and Owen. This copy of *Report to Greco*, Kazantzakis's great spiritual autobiography, published after his death, had been purchased by Dad in a bookseller's stall below the Parthenon while we were staying at the Hotel Plaka in Athens on January 8, 1977 — a fact which I can tell from a note he made in the inside front cover of the book. What you may not know is that — in the 'Prologue' to *Report*— Dad clearly marked a number of passages with the word 'Funeral.' Since I have long known and loved these passages myself, and since I have had his copy of the book since I moved to Laredo, I have always planned to read them at the service for him following his death. That time, of course, has come.

> I collect my tools: sight, smell, touch, hearing, intellect. Night has fallen. I return like a mole to my home, the ground. Not because I am tired. I am not tired. But the sun has set.

> ...To whom should I say farewell?... Where can I find an unyielding
> soul of myriad wounds like my own, a soul to hear my confession?
> Before you I shall pluck out the precious feathers of my jackdaw
> soul, one by one.... I shall relate my struggle to you.... Listen, there-
> fore, to my report, general, and judge. Listen to my life, grandfather,
> and if I fought with you, if I fell wounded and allowed no one to
> learn of my suffering, if I never turned my back to the enemy:
> Give me your blessing!"

With these closing words, I looked around at the small group of
people gathered there on an April afternoon. My love for them, to
adopt Kazantzakis's own phrasing, was flame and thorns. I turned
without comment from reciting Kazantzakis's words and abruptly
pressed the "play" button of the small cassette player on the table next
to me. A voice spoke strongly from the black Sony boom box. It was
not my voice, Father, but yours; dubbed and edited by John Hastings
and me from a master tape of my father reading from the Bible, a tape
I had persuaded him to make for me many years ago to preserve his
beautiful bass voice. My father spoke to us from the closing verses of
Ecclesiastes:

> Remember now thy Creator in the days of thy youth, while the evil
> days come not, nor the years draw nigh, when thou shalt say, I have no
> pleasure in them.... And the door shall be shut in the streets, when
> the sound of the grinding is low, and he shall rise up at the voice of
> the bird, and all the daughters of music shall be brought low; ... and
> the almond tree shall flourish, and the grasshopper shall be a burden,
> and desire shall fail.

The living sound of my father's voice, the unexpectedness of its
issuance, the familiar timbre of the sermon-like tone — to say nothing
of the definitive language which animates this greatest book of the Old
Testament — had visibly shaken the now-diminished family gathered
there. I had intended the contents of the Dolbyized, 90-minute cassette,
electronically encoded on ferromagnetic tape, to be like an arrow
pointed unerringly at our hearts. But once made from the shaft, it
entered the soul. How could it not? He was there among us, one last
time. My father's closing words I took as a direct exhortation to me:

And further, by these, my son, be admonished: of making many
books there is no end. And much study is a weariness of the flesh.

The service concluded shortly afterward. Drained and trembling,
I staggered around the corner of David's lovely home set in the mountains outside Bellingham, escaping the others. I leaned up against the
corner of the painted gray timbers and wept for the first time in two
days, suddenly and furiously and without hope, inhaling the cool air
of my beloved Pacific Northwest with relief, tasting the first new edge
of his disappearance.

I have written this frankly confessional opening in the form of a
parable drawn from my own life because it unites, in a pair of compelling episodes, themes common throughout this book and particularly to this chapter of my text. Aspects of experience — and thus a
deepening awareness of private wisdom — often cannot be neatly
walled off from each other, nor should they be. The stories above reflect
directly on the nature of learning, and the passions — both intellectual
and personal — which can impel and fortify it; how books, as physical
objects of great beauty, play a crucial role in such an unfolding; and
the way in which knowledge or the experience of art can become "per-
sonalized" (an issue which I will take up at greater length in the next
chapter).

Perceptive readers, however, will see at once the real intention
behind my account of Mahler's *Resurrection Symphony* and the dramatic quotation I played of my father reading from Ecclesiastes:
*Advanced, popular and increasingly affordable technology was intrinsic
to both episodes.* Some of our most profound aesthetic and personal
experiences now issue directly from such technology and would in fact
be categorically impossible to achieve without such scientific miracles
at our disposal. Without in any way detracting from the usefulness of
the book, who would dare to limit the human soul to enlightenment
only by "traditional" means? The scientific discovery of sound repro-
duction has literally shaped the texture of my own soul — and the souls
of all those with the imagination to listen deeply — as profoundly as
printed books. For all I know, they may dignify the solemnities of my
deathbed.

When I arrived at the Yeary Library ten years ago, not a single computer existed in Public Services. Ten years later, like every other library in the country, we are overflowing with them to such an extent that funding the expensive instruments is less a problem than retooling the guts of a library building which was never designed to provide electrical outlets and telecommunication ports into every nook and cranny where they're needed. The tidal wave of technology symbolized by the Internet — whose greatest national precedent really was not Arpanet but OCLC, although the rest of the country may never realize this — finally over-spilled the cataloging department onto the main floor of the library, and at this moment we are still in its explosive infancy. Over time, I expect there will be greater standardization of search screens; the current, unproductive plethora of state consortia which are springing up will get whittled down; traditional interlibrary loan will be utterly transformed or may disappear; and libraries will likely shrink significantly in size. These are just a few of the possible consequences.

Most exciting to me, as a scholar, will be the gradual unlocking of the world's vast treasure cave of archival materials. I have already perused, on the Web, stunning thirteenth century manuscripts from an archive in Seville — digitized images that even on my Model T of an IBM compatible I can click on and enlarge at will, refining the image so closely as to be able to discern the ripples in the parchment and the traceries of palimpsests underneath. The color seems as vivid as the original codex.

The bold release of the Dead Sea Scrolls a few years ago by the good folks at the Huntington Library, on microfilm, is but a harbinger of the archival liberation which is yet to come and which will inaugurate, I believe, a revolution in the humanities — liberating (for the first time ever) precious, fragile archival collections from the crypts they have necessarily been embalmed in for centuries. Scholars, even teenagers on fire for learning, may turn up lost Mozart quartets or fragments of precious texts by ancient authors believed lost forever. Who can tell? And as the Huntington precedent proved, access to such materials — scanned in and floating like stars in the sky of cyberspace and available to all — may circumvent the tendency of some scholars to hold onto "their" materials by opening up research to everyone. Surely such a democratizing influence is devoutly to be wished.

This period of information infancy, in short, very much resembles the cosmological Big Bang's first fractional moments, in which a comprehensive new order is exploding outward with unforeseeable results. The force of this radiating energy, spawned in the glowing microchips of late twentieth century techno-science, will offer to the future as many ramifying, unforeseen combinations as the Big Bang itself. And its social power matches the computing power of its increasingly potent machines. Computers have already reordered everything, as surely as did the agricultural revolution, the invention of fire and the discovery of the wheel. In the end, they will reorder everything except human nature.

The imperatives of the social sphere — the particular *individual* natures of the men and women who make it up and are asked to live together — have not changed since *Homo sapiens* solidified as a single, preeminent species. The computer has indeed revolutionized the workflow in our reference office, but it has not changed office politics. That feature of the office remains perennially the same: a warren of conflicting wills, friendships, passions, and endless cycles of interpersonal aggression and forgiveness. Alliances form and remain, alongside occasional hostilities. It is part of being human, our blessing and our curse.

Human interaction, in other words, is largely affective and emotional and more rarely rational, let alone "scientific." How else could *The Odyssey* or the Bible move us with their timeless parables about human nature? Odysseus, captive in a seeming paradise of Circe's creation, still longs for Penelope and the home the gods keep denying him. Even Circe's explosive and insistent sexuality — allied against the concept of the hearth which Penelope, of course, represents — cannot dissuade Odysseus from his tears of remembrance and this, touches all of us (perhaps especially husbands and fathers) who can read feelingly today, precisely because human personalities and the rip-tides of their interaction are the same today as they were in Homer's time, almost 3,000 years ago. This is one of the principal and most astonishing "laws" of meaning as they are to be found in the humanities; all the more astonishing because such vivid sympathies can and do survive all the incredible — one might think insurmountable — obstacles of botched translation across multiple languages, tremendous historical discontinuities, changing critical trends and the rise of radically different cultural assumptions. Homer is so humanly splendid his message can even survive an occurrence which would have terrified a hero like Odysseus far more than any Charybdis: a visit to the mall.

It is now clear that science and its handmaiden technology are linear in their development, and that political systems will operate to keep science going by driving the world toward global democracy and *its* ominous enchantress, unregulated capitalism. But the frail human heart is not linear; its beauties are cyclic and bounded by mortality, whose daily metaphor for each of us is sleep — presided over by the goddess Lethe each night. But, the computer, remorseless as the prurience of Circe the Enchantress, never sleeps. Cyberspace, the Internet, information technology: These are not benign tools in the traditional sense, anymore than Gutenberg's innocuous-looking, smudged bits of movable type were "mere" tools. The intractably lumpen wooden blocks he used to produce his incunabula were as unappealing aesthetically as my cumbersome IBM console: made of tawdry plastic, guaranteed for replacement (if funds are available, I am always assured) in another 18 months.

But what Gutenberg's sooty type fonts ended in, as we have seen, was the dissemination of literacy on an unprecedented scale, an event which, put in its simplest form, eventually led to the Enlightenment and the science-democracy-capitalist construct in which we, in the First World at least, now live and prosper. *This is the greatest good for the greatest number that has ever existed.* Science (inextricably dependent on democracy, widespread literacy and the free flow of information and knowledge working together) has halved the work week, freed us from the ravages of disease, reduced infant mortality and parent suffering, subdued populations elsewhere run amok and lengthened lifespans to problematic extremes. Science, in short, is the most successful human institution ever created — so superior to religion as a means of social organization it isn't funny.

The people of Gutenberg's time (like the students who are waiting for us in groups to open at 7:30 every morning) instantly recognized the utility of what had occurred in Gutenberg's poorly lit workshop in Mainz. The fireball flashed across Europe, despite all the impediments of rutted roads and tired donkeys. Gutenberg issued his famous Gutenberg Bible — a folio of 1,282 pages — in either 1456 or 1457. By 1463 the new process had already spread to Basel, Cologne and other major population centers in Germany. Just a year later, two Germans had set up a shop in Rome. The invention reached Paris in 1470, Holland in 1471, and Switzerland and Hungary in 1472 and 1473, respectively. England and Spain soon had presses of their own. It is as if European geography didn't exist, that the invention had neutered it. Now, 500 years later, in our library, anyone who can walk in the door can take a walk in cyberspace, where geography literally disappears. Full virtual reality will be here in the blink of an eye. In 30, 40 years? Who can say? We must speak of rates of change in six-month increments now.

The unshaven, ham-fisted butchers of Mainz, like their wives laying aside their tedious and interminable sewing, could not possibly have guessed where Gutenberg's invention would end, anymore than any of us can truly discern the long-term impact of the new information order we have just created. And one need not think that the butcher and his wife were intent on reading the Bible and Aristotle, the better to ponder "large" questions of time and fate. Far from it. A huge trade in tawdry Gothic chivalric romances soon sprang up across Europe, just as today's chatlines and e-mail dribble with all the ephemera English professors delight in decrying.

It has been one of the intentions of this book to provide, whenever possible, construals which are both universal and particular, and to keep in tantalizing suspension two colliding world views and two concurrent arguments. And if good technology — technology that has ennobled mankind, lifted our gaze, freed us from needless suffering — has a universal aspect, it also has a particular one, which must now be acknowledged.

Any reference librarian has stories. Stories in which the victory of helping a patron, student or faculty member suddenly makes the absurdities of an often obdurate higher administration worth enduring. So it has been with me. I think here of incidents like one I encountered last year with a history instructor at the college. In a conversation with me at the reference desk he happened to mention an old friend of his, a journalist he'd known in college back in Arkansas and hadn't seen for two decades. For years he'd tried directory assistance in various Arkansas cities as a means of locating his friend's phone number or address — all to no avail. Finally he had given up. As the instructor left for class, I took down the friend's name, telling him I'd like to follow up. Not five minutes later, I called him at his office. *People Finder* on the Web had given me several matches — including one in a small Arkansas town.

Another example: Many of our students struggle mightily with adventures in nascent literary criticism. The papers they are assigned often (sometimes too often, in my opinion) seem to be dry rehashes of the canonical heroes: Hawthorne, Poe, Fitzgerald, Hemingway, among the Americans. Recently, however, an English instructor threw us a curve ball (God bless him) and assigned an author who is not widely known. He had the class write about Margaret Fuller, Hawthorne's enigmatic contemporary and friend. All of the usual printed sources like the *Dictionary of Literary Biography* proved of little use; but our staff quickly located a wealth of growing information on the Internet, including the newly built Margaret Fuller Web Page.

What goes for students and faculty members goes for librarians, of course, even self-styled traditionalists like me. One of my least interesting duties I had before the advent of computers in public services was explaining to students how to use paper periodical indexes like *The Readers' Guide* effectively. The relationship between subject headings, citations and finding the articles in our periodicals collection always seemed to confuse them. Also, no matter how hard I might try to make these recitations interesting they always seemed to come off as needlessly complicated, boring, and — to my horror — increasingly canned. Sometimes, on a long tour of duty at the reference desk on a Monday night, I could hear my voice sinking into a singsong delivery. How could students not be bored? I was too. And yet the material was essential for them to comprehend.

Computers changed all that for me. With their plethora of full-text articles, the absolute miracle of Boolean searching (someone deserves the Nobel prize for that one) and with the advent of enlarged, easier-to-read onscreen citations and accompanying abstracts, the explanations I was able to give students about finding articles in our library became easier for me to make and for them to understand. Now, of course, with full-text capabilities, students are thrilled with the ease with which they can find materials.

Indeed, of all the computerized resources available to our students, the full-text CD-ROM or Internet-based magazine indexes seem to me to be the most useful, the biggest of all advances in librarianship thus far. Whereas the Internet can drown students in a plasma field of too much information, most students using an electronic version of *The Readers' Guide,* for example (and especially if they ask for help) will come away with a quantity of useful information. With the advent of push button printing and its real-time convenience, no wonder our student surveys have filled up with comments like "Thanks for the computers! Now I have more time to study." Or, "Before it took forever to find stuff. Now I can focus on my classes." It's a little hard to argue with successes of this kind. And, simply by observing the preference of our students to *completely avoid* interacting with the paper periodical collection if they can print the article, I can only conclude that paper periodicals may not exist in libraries, as such, in ten years — just as microfilm will, presumably, soon be gone as well, digitized into history and onto the Web.

Here, then, is the library transformed! Infinite access. A beacon of democratic hope. Seemingly endless possibilities for the advancement of learning, such as to make Francis Bacon himself set sail again from the New Atlantis. Surely the computer is the next best step in what Jacob Bronowski, a personal hero of mine, called so movingly the Ascent of Man.

Traditionalist librarians like me must freely and openly admit the virtues of the new information technology if any semblance of intellectual honesty — essential to debate — is to be maintained, or the subtlety of my doubts is to be appreciated. It is not surprising that machines endowed by their creators with such fabulous capabilities should have brought us to the point where we are: the rapid evolution of technology's now-iron grip on the entire profession of librarianship at every level. Technology now drives the budget. And it drives the cataloging, acquisitions, circulation, interlibrary loan and reference function as well. Technology dominates the journal literature in our field and the curricula of the graduate programs that train librarians. In the latter case, it has of course been often suggested in articles in major library publications that the words "library" or "librarianship" be *dropped* from the titles of our graduate studies programs, and from the degrees we award. In a world where the flashiness of the word "information" counts more than the fussy outdatedness of *mere* "librarianship" (and where the stereotypical Marian is always lurking somewhere in the background), no wonder our younger, increasingly male graduate students are urging a change. And yet, as a writer, I am alive to the implications of words and to their etymologies, which can often crystallize immensely complex and divisive issues.

The word "library," for example, comes from the Latin "librarium," for "bookcase"—hence also "librarianship." Tending books, then (the Latin for book, of course, being "liber") is the core of all that we do—and its active mode is, by extension, reading.

The invention of orthographic characters made human records possible, and thus written history (as opposed to the oral tradition, which otherwise spanned the entirety of organized human social existence) came into being with the advent of writing some 2,500 years ago. The beauty of the oral tradition, in which legend and poetry reigned, coalesced at last into social memory with the coming of the written Word.

As a historian, among the Greeks, Herodotus seemingly occupies both realms, mixing real events and people with fanciful (and invariably delightful) yarns. By the time of Thucydides, however, just a few decades later, the last vestiges of orality and legend had disappeared: the *Peloponnesian War*, though an absolute masterpiece by any standard, is starkly objective by comparison with Herodotus's *The Persian Wars*, and the "niceties" of poetry, legend and myth passed forever into the domain of "literature," where they have been locked away ever since. Homer—or at least those bards whom we call "Homer," who wrote down the epics ascribed to him—gave a fixity to the accounts of Odysseus and Achilles which, fortunately, preserved them for future generations. Indeed, they sit now on the shelves of my own "librarium" at home, by a route too improbable for fiction, because they were fixed in orthographic writing. What has been lost from our world, however — though it is still preserved for members of primitive, wholly "oral" societies even in the present day — was what must have been the stunning immediacy of the sung Bardic versions of Odysseus's encounters with "No Man," or his touching embarrassment before the beautiful maid Nausicaa, as he hid his nakedness, or (from the *Iliad*) Hector's moving farewell to his wife Andromache on the battlements of windy Troy.

Books levered one mode of human experience out of the narrative of the West and have increasingly channeled it toward literacy and reading, which has now become dominant for almost any educated person. Reading — the library its great symbol — became the heart of the university system as established in Europe in the Middle Ages; and even today one still goes "up" to Oxford to "read." Books, beautiful as I find them to be in a world where so much is now a simulation of real experience, are not to be worshipped in themselves, but achieve their formal cause only in the act of being opened, read and internalized (a theme I will take up at greater length in the next chapter). The immediacy of the Bard's sung poetry is echoed for us now in the dreaming flight of the imagination which deep reading provokes, especially among the young, where a passion for it, ideally, should take root.

We are now downwind, however — by a mere 40 years — of an invention which has done more, since its advent, to diminish reading, dumb down a populace, distract young minds, hobble their imagination at its root and claim their souls than any other in civilized human history. This device, of course, is television. And it's in every home in the known universe. Political parties, presidents and their mistresses, the institution of marriage, the nuclear family itself — these come and go, of course, but television will be with us forever. There's too much money in it for it to be allowed to disappear.

And I note that all of the same promises made for television in the 1950s — when it first hit the cities of the eastern seaboard and then spread outward like a fireball — are now being made for the Internet: it will enhance education. It will bring people closer. Its potential to improve us far outweighs its possible negative effects. Then, to flip modes, television's advocates began insisting that *not* to embrace it as all-redeeming was suspect. Old-fashioned. Heretical even. Television presaged a New World Order.

Yet is there a mind so perverse that could maintain that these promises for television, (especially as regards education,) have remotely been realized? Television has so eroded reading among most children today that educationally minded parents must fight battles of Gallipoli, or ban it from the home altogether, to focus their children's attention on developing lifelong relationships with books. Never mind that children routinely study with the TV on, or that this box is a glowing presence in most American homes above 40 hours per week — longer than the average workweek. Television, which is becoming ever more mindless, violent and needlessly explicit, is also among the most isolating technologies ever invented, nipping family interaction in the bud and substituting in its place separate "viewing experiences." As for television's benefits outweighing its faults, we have seen at best only fitful glimmerings of this possibility, generally on Public Television — chronically under-funded as it is.

In the broadest terms, the West (and thus, the world) moved from the oral tradition to the narrative tradition, and has now entered the visual tradition. If you don't believe this, watch any teenager for a 30-minute period. The teenager's world is almost entirely mediated by visual stimuli which are clever, seductive, irresistible and unending. A book simply has no chance before such stupendous power. Students will, grudgingly, read when required, and when such an effort is directed toward a clear end where there will be a profit for them (like a grade). But a voluntary, let alone ecstatic, "entering into" with a book has been slammed shut for them by media empires whose power and scale grow greater with each passing day, and who know very well the impact they are having.

The Internet, of course, is only one part of the information revolution in libraries, but at my back I hear the horns and motors of some dreadful, subtle misconstrual on the part of nearly every librarian I talk to. I believe we must be cautious of the actual intellectual value, not only of what students are retrieving but of the increasing isolation in which they are retrieving it. I believe we must be skeptical of any concept of "speed" and "efficiency" as it applies to any aspect of education. And I am certain that the focus required for reading a book — which paradoxically liberates the imagination — in no way resembles the fixed stare of students and patrons locked into a highly interactive "medium" that, all too often, and even for experienced searchers, degenerates into mere surfing.

Pardon me for signaling the need for caution, for a correction in the profession and, if nothing else, for more heated debate than I think is currently occurring. Pardon me for suggesting that, useful though online indexes, the Internet and other electronic resources *can* be (as I have admitted), they are useful only when used with circumspection and precision and that, even then, they remain under the domain of *information* and not *knowledge*, and that it must always be the latter which has priority in librarians' views of themselves, their patrons and their profession.

Let's take an example. (Examples happen to me now all the time.) Her name was Cynthia. When she came to me, she told me she had been searching for *two days* on the Internet before someone had told her to seek me out. What she needed, she explained, was a well-researched biography of Henry VIII — longer and more comprehensive than most general encyclopedia articles, but not a book-length treatment. She was, she told me, at her wits' end and time was running out before her presentation tomorrow. As I stepped over to the reference stacks and handed her volume nine of the *Dictionary of National Biography,* with its splendid entry on Henry VIII, we began to talk. I explained the virtues of the *DNB*, and its American equivalent, the *Dictionary of American Biography,* and we discussed at greater length that the difficulty here had been her already settled conviction that "everything's on the Net." This, she told me, had been her general impression from television and even from some of her instructors.

Cynthia and I also discussed copyright issues and how they often bear a direct relationship with what is available on the Web — and that you must often pay for valuable information. No doubt, I told her, something comparable to the *Dictionary of National Biography*'s entry on Henry VIII was "out there," but I encouraged her always to ask for assistance from one of our staff to see if we might not get it quickly from the reference collection, free of charge and in moments.

What worries me as much as Cynthia's misunderstanding of the Web's current capabilities, or her lack of understanding of how to search to find information effectively, is a phenomenon I've already noticed, just in the relatively short time the Internet has been available in our library. This concern falls into two parts: the concept of self-directedness and the quality of the questions I have lately been receiving from students as I log my hours at the reference desk each day.

The idea of a library as a "librarium," or collection, evolved over the centuries to include also the idea of a caretaker, a librarian, who at first was chiefly an organizer and a cataloger of materials, but who now plays the more active role of a helper, or even at times a surrogate teacher. The librarian serves the patron or student by "referring" to the collection himself, or by pointing the way to answers. For those of us who take our chief joy in this role, or, indeed, entered the profession because of it, such a responsibility, as every reference librarian knows, is both daunting and immensely rewarding. I like to think that any good reference librarian, in the deepest sense, humanizes the collection. Ideally, he or she should embody the virtues of learning and the principles of scholarship and reading. No single librarian can perfectly sustain such a role every hour of every day, of course, and we all have strengths or weaknesses in various subjects. But one of the difficulties I have with technology is that the very self-directedness librarians and automation vendors have been crowing about as some great good (increasingly easy-to-use screen prompts, real-time printing of articles, ramifying hyper-text links) means that we reference librarians are being further and further distanced from patrons who before would have sought our help. As a colleague of mine recently noted, "Maybe we should just disable the 'Help' screens. Then they'll be forced to ask us for the help they need."

It never occurred to Cynthia, who was in serious trouble, to turn to one of us for assistance, even though we were in plain sight for the entire two days she said she was "drowning." Cynthia's "self-directedness," which postmodern librarianship manifestly encourages (in unexamined obedience, I fear, to the big database manufacturers and vendors who want our money) was actually detrimental to her needs. And what were those needs? The simplest of all possible needs: a thorough, though brief, entry on England's most famous monarch. In a reversal whose implications should seriously frighten every reference librarian, Cynthia simply never thought to ask. After a financial investment in our library for a vast new automation system totaling nearly one million dollars, in a library now able to boast that it had "infinite access," Cynthia almost fell through the cracks. And even though it may be argued that in the past, in non-automated libraries, patrons did so too, it must nevertheless be chastening — and a factor which gives perspective to our thinking about technology — that a fully automated one is no necessary guarantee against such mishaps, despite the huge sums of money involved.

A second concern has surfaced out of the web of general impressions which I have formed in interacting with our students since the advent of high technology in our library. Their questions are chiefly of a technical nature now. They involve problems like the terminals freezing up, the need to reload paper, the briefest of explanations to new users about how to log on and begin basic searching. The students who do ask me questions have all the certainty, intentionality, and absorption of anyone at a computer screen — none of the searching, sometimes confused look of students requiring assistance in the reference stacks who are easy to spot and easy to help. Breaking through the Internet searcher's rapt, attention-filled love affair with that screen, for me — as a librarian charged to help them — presents a challenge parents will recognize when they try to come between their offspring and a TV show. Except that this experience is supposed to be about education, not extraterrestrials.

Is it any surprise that the quality and the depth of the questions I receive from students locked on the Internet have shrunk chiefly to trouble-shooting the printer? There is very little that is human or humane in this glittering setting, in which, because lines are long and time-limits are monitored, a sense of urgency pervades the entire reference experience. The creation of our "new" library was a necessity driven by student and faculty demands, the need to meet mandatory accreditation criteria, the college's desire to remain up-to-date, and the library administration's obligation to open up new and potentially redeeming experiences for our students. But we must also recognize that no utopia has been created and that few of the basic issues of real education have been effectively addressed. Our students' ability to combine the data they've downloaded or printed out ("information") into linkages of thought and opinion ("knowledge") and then write a paper skillful enough to express real insight is still absolutely dismal, according to every English instructor I've talked to. And according to some, it's getting worse. Only a close association with words — simple reading and writing — can ever remedy this.

Sometimes a frightening vision comes to me — dreamlike and inescapable — that the student or patron is now the extension of the lurid, unsleeping *machine*, and not the reverse; that we — all of us — are becoming as interchangeable as the girl in the undignified paper hat at McDonald's who takes my order, where what is important (for sales) is not real emotion but feigned friendliness. The "library without walls" with its Circean promise of "infinite access" — I suddenly realize — was just a front for the money, a front for Microsoft, or DRA or Innovative; just as my belated love of democracy is now just a front for the greed-soaked capitalism of the postmodern era, which is what is really driving all the smug talk of a "new globalism" by businessmen in bespoke suits flipping open their laptops on the Concorde.

The students pressing the <enter> keys in our library — I shudder to think — their faces eerily up-lit with the cobalt blues of the radiant screens, have been misplaced in a sea of adult unawareness. Illiteracy rates in the border community in which I live run as high as 48 percent, according to national surveys. There is not for this generation even the relative idealism of the sixties and early seventies, when we read *Steppenwolf* and *Siddhartha* into the night. And our library, like the *Victoria's Secret* catalog, has been transformed, in the exact space of the decade I've worked here, into a wilderness of exotic choices. Access without focus. Information without knowledge. Choice without context, directionless and ubiquitous as the sea.

It is not for librarians to say, "We did it to get the status we never had." Not enough for us to claim "everybody wanted it." Our pursuit of technology as an end in itself promises no certain utopia and will provide no certain answers. And we have barely begun to discuss the real impact on our patrons and students these changes foretell, or on some of our profession's most hallowed traditional values. The sacred *logos* cannot survive the profane LAN, because the context by which knowledge could subdue information has been shattered.

What a different experience when a student like Cynthia comes to me at the reference desk with a confession of need and, in a kind of friendship, we can go to actual shelves and take down actual, tangible volumes and open pages and read across to find answers — or not find them, and begin again the search which, in miniature, is the story of every quest to know something.

I didn't stop with Cynthia, you see, when I handed her volume nine of the *Dictionary of National Biography*. I took her question as an opportunity, a point of contact. I mentioned to her as we looked at the entry that the scholars who compiled this set, which took decades to complete, were all biographers and historians of impeccable credentials — and that just to be asked to contribute to the *DNB* was a kind of life honor for them. And that although she would do well to also read a more contemporary encyclopedia article on Henry VIII to cover recent research, she could rely on the scholarship of the *DNB* despite our volumes looking "old."

Cynthia raised the further issue of the "Church of England thing" and I explained a little of what I knew about it, confessing my own ignorance about many of the details. But we talked about the concept of the Reformation, its English manifestation, Henry's dissatisfaction with Catharine of Aragon's inability to bear him a son, the whole miasma with the Pope — we talked for maybe 15 minutes about some very salient facts of English history.

I realized that Cynthia had pieces of this puzzle but many of them weren't coherently linked, and I also realized the *Dictionary of National Biography* would set most of that to rights. It looked like we had "saved" her presentation after all.

The interplay of the student and the librarian, which is a mode of education, can be assisted by a computer, but it must not be replaced by one. No one but a librarian, who values and cares for students, could have accomplished this interaction as effectively, instructing and encouraging the student as it proceeded. It is a profoundly human point of contact, and both student and librarian can draw inspiration from it. Occasionally students I've helped will honor me by asking me to write recommendations for them as they apply for scholarships or admission to other schools — and *all* of these requests, all of these friendships, originally grew out of reference interviews just like the one with Cynthia. The "information"— the facts or statistics or data — I took as merely the starting point for a kind of conversation directed to something like scholarly ends. I attempt always to point beyond the particular to the general, moving from information to what is actually important: knowledge itself.

I have noticed that since the widespread introduction of technology in our library I am increasingly entombed — embalmed — in seemingly endless meetings about either information "systems" and "automation" or, more recently, "consortia" (another unlovely word), the latter of which seem to be springing up like toadstools everywhere. The sums of money "allocated" by "the legislature" to "promote information literacy" to "library end users" absolutely boggles the mind. *Tens of millions* of dollars have recently been bursting out of legislative pipelines in our state, all designed around the concept of complete access to every particle of information in the known universe. Rarely are any of these dollars earmarked for "traditional" materials — like books. *Never,* it seems, are any of these dollars earmarked for another kind of "traditional" material: librarians. In our library we are chronically understaffed, especially at the professional level, where we are below ACRL standards for professionals by 50 percent. In a recent editorial by a Texas Library Association president in *Texas Library Journal,* the president noted with jubilation that monies for technology were flowing and we had better all get on the bandwagon, and then lamented a little bit later in the piece that some 1,200 schools in Texas have no librarian at all on staff. I can only ask: What's wrong with this picture?

The core of my heresy, so painfully obvious both to myself and others, is this. Let me whisper it to you: *I don't care about "consortia." I've never even met one.* I only care about Cynthia, or Roberto, or

57

Reymundo or Alice. Encouraging them, assisting them, helping to translate their hopes into reality even in a small way, is the only duty I have ever set myself. I am deeply, unrepentantly *marginal*. I serve a truth which has increasingly alienated me from my colleagues and the administration with each public venture into print I have chosen to make. But I have never felt marginal to the students or the faculty I serve. The latter, especially those in English studies, understand instantly what I am talking about relative to the ability of technology to erode the learning process. They rightly see the Internet, especially, as being merely on a continuum with television, whose baleful effects they encounter in the classroom every day.

The best students I have encountered, of course, are the compulsive readers, the ones always with a book in hand. Generally such habits will extend back to early childhood, but among young people not gifted with extraordinary parents to oversee such a development, voracious reading is a thing of the past. One of our century's most daunting readers, the literary critic Harold Bloom, has underscored this decline in his great work, *The Western Canon:* "Unfortunately nothing will ever be the same because the art and passion of reading well and deeply, which was the foundation of our enterprise, depended upon people who were fanatical readers when they were still small children."

Bloom's comments have recently been weighing on me more and more as my misgivings have grown about the too-easy ethical neutrality of postmodern librarians about the new McLibrary we've put in place. He's led me to look at the quality of the lives, not of the outstanding students (whose habits of reading and steady application are securely in place), but at the middle-of-the-road students who show up at our terminals each day. True, they will conduct "research" of a sort, without ever asking me for help. But then, in our lab, they'll jump, as quickly as they can, into their e-mail accounts or onto a chatline, where they will linger in some cases for hours. The length of such marathon sessions is almost unbelievable. What *could* they be talking about? I have no idea. If the lab is full, they'll sit waiting. They wait interminably for terminals, their textbooks closed.

The reading of a book is an entirely different sort of passivity. Reading is, properly, a kind of leisure. It is, ideally, unhurried. It is, one might say, deeply passive because it is imaginative, yet still focused. Not so an online experience, which is not passive but highly interactive and constantly, inappropriately stimulating. It encourages surfing and thus the disruption of narrative sequence, ending in the actual reduction of focus — precisely what a book will not, indeed cannot, do.

It is necessary now to turn to the subject of education, the origin of the range of educational values from which libraries must take their cue. What one finds there, regrettably, are inverted priorities, misguided sophistries and yet further evidence of fundamental values in disintegration.

Chapter 3

Good Education, Bad Education

The stars, inlaid in the night sky like patens of bright gold, shone above us. The members of our rhetoric class lay stretched out on the lawn below the university's campanile there on Mount Oread. It was almost 11 o'clock at night. Every 15 minutes, the bell of the campanile announced the quarter-hour while we watched the stars wheel above us and heard the lecture. Strong Hall, the administrative building, showed as a block of dark set against the luminous night sky. Cars from Jayhawk Boulevard, which curved in front of Strong Hall, were scarcely audible to us here on this part of the Hill, as it was called, which sloped down toward the pond and its ancient stone footbridge. Rachel, a sophomore in the program with whom I was hopelessly in love, was telling the stories of intrepid kings and rescued daughters, of hunters brave and serpents dangerous, of all the heroes slain in battle.

"There is Cepheus the King," Rachel was saying. "See the five bright stars in the shape of a pentagram? Now the myth is that Cepheus, and his queen, Cassiopeia...."

I stole a glance at Rachel's profile in the starlight. I was convinced I had never seen anything as rare, as perfect, as lovely, on this earth.

"And since they did not get along, she is placed, you see, across the sky from him. See the 'W' over there?" Suddenly she paused. "Bill, are you getting this?"

Oh my God, I thought wildly. She knows. She must have seen me watching her! And now she'll hate me.

I replied as best I could.

"Uh..."

"Well," Rachel said to me, as the rest of the class exchanged glances, "Why don't you tell us about Orion, then."

"Uh, yes. Orion. The hunter. Had a shield."

"What kind?"

"A ... a ... tiger skin."

"*Lion*-skin shield," Rachel interrupted.

"Yes. Lion. Winter constellation — God, I'm sorry ... he fought —" I frowned in fierce concentration — "he was blinded by Dionysus, out of jealousy!" I blurted out. (How appropriate, I thought — a man blinded by the god of sensuality for looking at a beautiful woman at the wrong time.)

We watched the stars awhile longer, as the surface temperature of my face began to cool, and then the students gradually dispersed in the direction of the dorms. Before leaving, Rachel took me aside and commented, "Your connection of Orion to Dionysus was actually pretty good. Most don't know they're in any way related. The 'jealousy' part comes in with a strain of the myth related to Artemis, however. See you Monday."

The Integrated Humanities Program of which Rachel and I were both students was a two-year "Great Books" program at the University of Kansas, which flourished in the 1970s and into the mid–1980s. Nothing like it had existed before then at any American university; nothing like it has existed since. Not at St. Johns. Not today at Columbia. And, now that its unique, controversial voice has been silenced, not at Kansas. The program, which simply sought — as its director Dennis Quinn said — to "teach the humanities as the humanities," attracted controversy like a magnet when it was discovered that its three major professors were Catholic, and rumors of Catholic indoctrination began to spread. As a student in the program for all four semesters, and a non–Catholic — indeed an agnostic humanist — I can attest that such a frenzy of concern was ill founded and mystifying. And although it was obvious that Professors Quinn, Nelick and Senior, who presided over the main lectures twice a week, were informed by a strong Catholic faith, such concerns never made it into the classroom. Something else did, though. Something indefinable. Something poetic — like patens of bright gold strewn unaccountably across the night sky.

The deep structure of the Pearson Program (as those of us who knew it in its early days still call it, when it was housed in Pearson Hall) was, of course, the Great Books, which were read — the Bible was the only exception — in their entirety, and, of course, in translation. Spanning the freshman and sophomore years, the program also included weekly rhetoric classes, which expanded on the long, twice-weekly lectures given by the professors; stargazing, as a means of teaching students the Greek myths; a formal Spring Waltz, funded and put on by the students, and which became legendary on campus for sheer gallantry and romance; workshops in calligraphy; a country fair, held by Pearson students in the autumn, which raised money for the waltz; a two-year, optional program in oral Latin; and a comprehensive, two-year poetry memorization component, which was required of all students. Songs — usually Irish ballads — were sung by the class before each lecture, and the program even had an insignia and motto to help it thread its way through the surrounding multiversity, which viewed all this either as nonsense or with bafflement.

The insignia was, in visual miniature, a distillation of the entire program's intentions as Dennis Quinn, Frank Nelick and John Senior had framed them. An image of the Big Dipper was set against a deep blue, circular field of the night sky. It pointed unerringly to the pole star, representing truth, at which all education must aim as its proper end. Around the circular shield ran a quilted braid of gold, like the band which bounds the Shield of Achilles — one of the most important readings of the course, from *The Iliad* — representing the mighty Stream of Ocean, and delimiting the cosmos, perhaps within some greater law than we can know. The program asked questions. Are we bounded merely by our own desires? What is the nature of the good life? What is the meaning of a person's daily labor? What is journeying? What is home? Such questions lay at the heart of the poetic, and therefore highly suggestive, mode of knowledge which the professors were seeking.

Real truths always unfold themselves over a lifetime. Nelick, Senior and Quinn not only knew this, they wanted to enshrine such a set of wonderings as the core of the enterprise in which they were engaged. The program's motto was *Nascantur in Admiratione*: "Let Them Be Born in Wonder."

To this day, I don't know if the truth about life is that it is safely "bounded" by some transcendence I can always and everywhere rely on. The program simply set me to thinking about it, wondering about it, pondering its deep meaning, over the years — as losses and victories in my life have waxed and waned, as my parents began to die and my children began to be born, or as I passed from school into the life of work, or as my commitment to creativity strengthened despite an inherently pessimistic nature. Insofar as the Great Books deal with these questions, the Kansas farm boys and girls who fell into the program were gradually raised out of their complacency and middle-class expectations and elevated to a new eminence of vision. Kids who would never have cracked open Homer on their own were, as if by some rare magic, soon devouring the pages of *The Iliad* and *The Odyssey*, Plato's *Republic*, Herodotus' *Persian Wars*, Thucydides' *Peloponnesian War* and the Greek myths as rendered by Ovid. We plowed through Virgil's *Aeneid*, Caesar's *Gallic Wars*, Plutarch's tremendous *Lives*, the Bible's most notable sections, Augustine's *Confessions*, *The Song of Roland*, Geoffrey Chaucer's merry *Canterbury Tales*, Cervantes' peerless *Don Quixote*, several plays by Shakespeare, and more besides.

In groups of eight or ten students, we memorized whole poems of Wordsworth, Shelley, Keats, Hopkins, Yeats, Byron — and, in our final semester, mastered the entire *Elegy in a Country Churchyard* by Thomas Gray, all 130 imperial lines. Poetry began to live inside of us, because we could now quote from it — not only from our memories, but from our hearts. It began to make possible the most personal kind of possession of the world. No longer, for us — and never again — would the university campanile sounding the time be simply a device to mark the hour; by extension its sound was a kind of calling and summoning, a summoning which in fact, the lectures revealed, underlies much of the narrative content of the West. And when one is summoned, and one leaves home, does not one long someday to return? "There is nothing worse for mortal men than wandering!" Odysseus cries.

Such a poetic approach to education is so intensely relevant to young people, who are beginning a journey, that it makes the usual mode of "studying" poetry, and amassing critical "data" on it, beggarly by comparison. Indeed, as Quinn pointed out in his essay "Education by the Muses,"

> The humanities have lost their allure because they have thrown away that which constitutes their distinctive appeal. I mean the love of knowledge for its own sake. To put it still more emphatically, the humanities have sold their heritage for a mess of methodology. The humanities have been professionalized and scientized to the point where the ordinary undergraduate with a budding love of poetry or history or art finds his affection returned in the form of footnotes, research projects, bibliographies, and scholarly jargon — all the poisonous paraphernalia that murders to dissect.

The "lectures" were not lectures at all. Students did not take notes nor ask questions. The three professors, sitting in front of the class, conducted an extended "conversation" among themselves, to which the students — perhaps 200 in number — were asked to *listen* deeply and meditatively. The conversations among the three professors were, moreover, deliberately unplanned and unrehearsed and therefore never the same from semester to semester. Their comments were guided, rather, by some aspect or nuance of the book being read which had struck the professors in their own rereading or contemplation of the text; or which may have been suggested by a student in the frequently intense discussions after class. Details of the text could well turn out to be significant — the thong which latched a door in *The Odyssey;* the use of the word "jocund" in a poem by Thomas Gray and its etymological implications; a discussion of a seemingly minor character, like Palinurus in *The Aeneid*, which, we discovered, provoked from Virgil some of the most profound lines of poetry in the entire epic. Any of these poetic moments could be a starting point for the conversation at the front of the class, which unrolled with such intrinsic interest, good humor and intellectual beauty that — within a few weeks — the entire class was welded to this new vision of education, one that none of us had ever experienced before. One in which delight and laughter were enthroned as an ideal, in which merriment could suddenly turn into the deeply profound; a vision of things where sadness and joy lay down together in meaning. Young people are inherently idealistic — they *want* romance, they *want* idealism, they *want* honor, purpose, meaning, continuity, the ability to trust adults above all. Young people are, indeed, primed for all these things. That our society so frequently denies them this sustenance is proven inversely by their delight when it is offered to them in its real form. And this was the secret of the Pearson Program: its assumption was not simply that all men desire to know. The program demonstrated convincingly that their desire to know comes from the delight encountered in the knowing and this is what propels education at every level. The professors stated repeatedly that the students were not "memorizing" poetry, they were *doing* poetry.

As Nelick pointed out in his essay "The Darkling Plain of Poetry," modern "scholarship" concentrates on the relationships between words and not things, whereas all poetry is properly grounded in things. The professors deftly removed the students' traditional dependence on written words — the distraction of notetaking, grammar books to study Latin (it was all memorization) or printed copies of the poems to be memorized. The poems we memorized (and there were dozens of them) were learned by responsory repetition in groups: the second-year student teaching us would say a line, from his or her own memory, and we would repeat it, again and again, until, within a week or two we had the whole poem by heart. This emphasis on doing carried over into the directness of stargazing, where we *saw* the stars, *heard* (not read) the myths, and then began to realize (with a great, inner dawning) that *we* had a connection — active and passionate — with the beauty and mystery of the stars. This gymnastic, participatory mode of education also underlay the calligraphy we learned, the apple cider we made at the country fair, the waltzing we mastered, the songs we sang before each lecture. These are very much childish things, of course, entirely and deliberately pre-scientific. Poetry, as Quinn, Nelick and Senior liked to say, is a *first* thing.

Education for each of us up to that point had been an accumulation of the means of knowledge — facts, delivered to us in scripted lectures, memorized without passion, regurgitated on an exam. Students can get very good at this, of course, as every teacher knows; I was good at them myself. But the brightest ones, rewarded continually, may know a great deal about the means of knowledge, and nothing about its ends. In the Humanities Program, poetry — and education in the poetic mode as I experienced it there — was very much about the ends of knowing, indefinable, irreducible, mysterious and no-man-fathomed (to use Hopkins's phrase) as these things necessarily are. At the very point where so much of modern educational or critical theory seeks to make the humanities explicit and clearly bounded so it can be neatly rendered into a student "paper," the Pearson Program deliberately sought to shroud poetry in mystery, opacity and awe.

No test question–type answers were ever provided. One day, a fellow classmate of mine, a quiet (one sensed brilliant) young woman with short dark hair and bangs, asked Dr. Quinn a question in one of the rhetoric classes which has stayed with me ever since. In *The Aenead*, at the famous Gate of Dreams, one gate is made of ivory, the other of horn. "Why would Virgil say," the girl inquired, "that one gate was made of ivory, and the other was made of horn?" Quinn, deeply impressed, (I could tell) with her close reading of the text as well as her sense for the mysterious, answered simply, "I have no idea." That she had recognized something *unexplainably* meaningful was the reason Quinn — normally diffident and quite "closed" emotionally — could scarcely conceal his admiration.

Within such a context for the humanities (the poetry, literature, philosophy and history which we read) it becomes possible, for the first time, to ascend without embarrassment to the real questions (the ones current education is afraid to deal with), the great categories of human meaning — the True, the Good, the Beautiful. Honor, justice, happiness, the good life. Leisure, vocation, work, pleasure, virtue. And, conversely, to illuminate evil, betrayal, prurience, fear. For the undergraduate, who is very much in the process of sorting these out in the dormitory, the cafeteria, the sorority and the classroom, the success of the Integrated Humanities Program, which lasted at Kansas for almost 15 years, was its frank confrontation of these categories of experience.

The result of teaching in this poetic mode, when allied to the strong personalities of the three professors, produced in the students a fierce devotion to the program such as I have never seen before or since. The Spring Waltz was the students' invention — an offspring of the concepts of gallantry, chivalry and romance lauded in readings from Chaucer to Cervantes. And the energy which the students put into the endeavor was little short of amazing. All the invitations (hundreds in number) were addressed by the students with the calligraphy we learned. The students — the young men as well as the young women — organized waltz lessons in church basements scattered throughout the city in the weeks prior to the big event. The student union ballroom was rented out with funds we raised, the university orchestra pressed into service.

The women bought or made formal dresses, the men (some of whom didn't even own a pair of black oxford shoes) rented tuxedos for the evening. One year, a couple famously arrived at the door of the Kansas Union in a coach and horse. In the ballroom, splendidly appointed, flowers decorated all the tables where the parents, professors and other guests sat, and on which had been placed poems about spring-time, likewise scripted in calligraphy. I myself helped construct a large white trellis filled with flowers, which provided a canopied entrance to the ballroom. And, in one of the most terrific honorings of my life, the prettiest young woman in the program consented to be my partner.

Julie and I had had long, serious discussions about the program's aims together and had grown to be friends, and my invitation seemed natural. Only later did I learn, to my astonishment, that every other man in the program had wanted to ask her to go, but none had been able to muster the courage. As Julie Ann and I twirled about the ball-room filled with beautiful couples I did choose something like a star; I did learn how to adore, admire, to be filled with awareness of another's smallest inflections of voice, scent, modesty. The romance of it all was overwhelming. How sentimental this may sound, how trite or nostalgic in description — how improbable such "ends" may seem compared with the important matters of educational "means." Young people today have sex, but what they want is the romance. What they want, precisely, is to be able to believe in another that much.

In that enterprise students were not numbers — we were often shocked when one of the professors, out of a class of 200, might suddenly call on us by name. Laughter in the lectures was spontaneous and unaffected. And, moreover, standards were high: very few "A"s were ever awarded. John Senior has written that the end of education is a species of love. It is also, he has said, a species of friendship. The program's concepts of honor, integrity, and the principled scholarly life were a calling we could not resist, and only now that it is gone, can we remember it as the shining moment it was.

One of the central mysteries of the program was the three professors themselves, who seemed to embody its aims. And although this no doubt annoyed them no end, they were the subjects of endless speculation among the students: we could scarcely conceal our admiration. The differences and lineaments of their various personalities (Quinn, diffident; Senior, meditative; Nelick, irascible though brilliant) spawned heated conversations in dorm rooms, apartments and coffee shops all over Lawrence. Part of this was that they spoke so rarely about themselves, their affections or their pasts. I cannot imagine three people more uninterested in anyone's perception of them. That they had all known each other for a long time was clear. It was also evident that they did not want to be called by their first names — that "Doctor" was *de rigueur* in their classroom. Predictably, such reticences soon endowed the professors with something of the mythic, fueling curiosity. But at some point, for all of us, mere curiosity began to give way to enduring respect. Mark Van Doren has said that the student secretly wants to respect the professor all along, even when he is resistant. The very formality of address which the professors demanded, their lack of a chummy "confessional" mode (so common in other classrooms on campus during the 1970s), and a singular concentration on the details of the books being read, ironically produced the very conditions of friendship by which superlative education occurs. No one imagined we were on "equal" terms with the professors — only that this "conversation" of theirs we were listening to was a method of instruction which was genial, affectionate, serious at times, and well intentioned. Song, laughter, jokes, gibes directed by the professors at each other, all played a part in the 90-minute lectures which, for me, were never long enough. I never knew from one minute to the next if I would be laughing, singing, or fighting back tears.

I can only conclude that the moral teacher, writ large, is, along with the subject matter, the second element of successful education. By "moral" I mean simply one who loves the truth. Who stands for learning. Who is not a counterfeit scholar. I do *not* mean by "moral" that he or she be "nice," or a prude or of any particular political persuasion. The best teachers I have had have been iconoclasts, or eccentrics, often irascible, always endearing. Each one has been emphatically an *individual*. It is like true poetry. It is not simply about sunny ends, fulfilled promises, the certainty that all will be well. No, it can also be an abyss, fearful, a darkling plain pitched in grief. The Pearson Program broached this poetic reality, too. None of the professors imagined they were engaged merely in entertaining middle-class, upwardly mobile teenagers with songs and little poesies. They were engaged, and they knew it, in an activity more subversive than making bombs. The introduction of art into one's life is perilous — it enlarges the soul, sometimes dangerously. It can make heartbreaks palpable and concrete in bitter ways, and give a face to horror as well as joy. Poetry, knowledge, meaning — these are crucifixions, as torturing as faith, yet without which life is not worth living.

The professors, for their efforts, earned the envy, calumny and dismissal of their university peers. Their Catholic faith was derided and held suspect, and the program never was able to escape the fact that much of its philosophy was medieval in origin and Catholic in tone. That a small number of students did actually convert to Catholicism was enough, apparently, in the minds of nervous university administrators, and some parents, to launch a full-scale investigation. And although it was deemed perfectly acceptable on that campus for feminist or muliticulturalist or Marxist professors to conduct classes openly tinged by their own political beliefs, the idea of a program that was supposedly subverting the sacred foundations of Midwestern Protestantism was too much to be born.

Quinn, as director, bore the brunt of the public humiliation of the "hearings." But the program was never the same, and a quiet bureaucratic disassembly from above began. Within a few years the entire edifice had crumbled, and the program that taught us to adore the stars was no more. I have never trusted adults, especially administrators, since.

In the years following my involvement with the program, the "uni"-versity has become still more splintered and politicized, and today the "ordinary undergraduate with a budding love for poetry or art or history" now confronts a curriculum not unlike the stupefying array of database choices available to that student upon entering our library.

I have seen with my own eyes that our young are desperately, searchingly, tragically hungry for an education exactly like the one I had the sheer blind luck to fall into with the Pearson Integrated Humanities Program. Quite apart from the splintered families, or the dead or dying religious impulse, the democracy itself is buckling beneath the strain of runaway capitalism and the rampant consumerism it invented. Our young long for idealism, romance, chivalry. They have received, all too often, mere relativism, sexuality without love, and the prostitution of their best impulses.

The frightening advent of the gang reveals this. The gang is a violent, inverted parody of the larger society grounded in barbaric adolescent sexuality and violence — but it is held together by strong codes of honor, loyalty, bravery and identity: within the tribe a sudden, still orderliness based upon strong philosophical principles obtains, whose logic its members could not possibly articulate, but which is no less real. Outside the tribe, God help us, lies everyone else.

Indeed, the gang presents a more coherent unity than the high school it terrorizes. It has generated philosophically respectable, even hallowed, categories impressively constructed in the wake of adult abandonment, selfishness and failure — and employed them to obviously unpardonable ends. There is a cry which I hear, particularly in its young members who are not yet hardened. This is why so many young gang members respond so quickly when placed in systems of corresponding order, hierarchy and loving authority and given direction by strong, unequivocal mentors.

What goes for the extremes of the gang, I have found, goes equally well for much of our youth. Our schools have failed to offer them a coherent view of the world, the purposes of knowing, or the role of education in their lives and the direction that gives. Their teachers are often shaky on all these points. "Means" are taught, but none of the "ends" which make them cohere. Many teachers are not passionate readers themselves. A great show may be made of reading, as I find it is in the schools here where I live, but the teachers, one can tell, are going through a pantomime prescribed by the administration.

When I talk with them, and ask a few pointed questions, I discover that they've read very little indeed and have not reflected deeply on it. Indeed, I have met only one exception here. He was voted Teacher of the Year for the district in his very first year, electrifying his high school class by having them read great works of history and philosophy, including *The Republic*, the works of John Locke, and *The Federalist Papers*. Richard told me one day at the local supermarket that he was stunned, when he mentioned to a middle-level district administrator that his eleventh graders were reading John Locke in the original, that the administrator had never heard of John Locke and had no idea who he was. Forty years of television, plus the non-subject education degree, had done its work on *his* brain.

Which brings me to the central point: Computers will not save education. In Aristotelian terms, they are neither necessary nor sufficient conditions. More money will not save it, as education is currently practiced. More databases in libraries won't save it, or the Internet in every classroom. Imbecilic workshops certainly won't save it. Even the common sense of national tests won't be enough now. *Only reading can save it.* That's the only thing — by both students (when they are children and ever after) and their teachers, starting today.

The whole nation will essentially have to start somewhere near ground zero. A victory, if it comes, will be won one page at a time, pages turned in silence and concentration; or in stories read from the pages of *The Wind in the Willows* or told out of the imagination of one's mother or father; or by vehement arguments over a "real" book in the hallways of high schools; or by following the example of the one imperial teacher we are ever to have who sets a level of expectation for ourselves higher than we thought we could achieve, and then puts us in sight of the goal. Notice the strong involvement of the adult at every level — parent and teacher both guide, monitor, inspire and provoke. In such a process not only is reading valorized as a natural good; the concept of reading and nurturance is implicitly reinforced.

The forces arrayed against such an effort are so staggering and well-funded that they may very well defeat any such parochial, grassroots attempt to overcome them. With the advent of television, and following cinema's glamorous lead, the cults of celebrity which fashion, provoke and refine consumer lust began in earnest. The celebrities themselves, as the media moguls who both invent and then dethrone them well know, are unimportant mayflies in themselves, except as the avatars of taste. As conduits for selling things, however, images are far more effective than anything in print. And so the entire foundation of American cultural experience has been deftly shifted from one based on print (or narrative) to one based on a stream of unending video images. The *context* for reading is gone, and the CEOs in their cordovan shoes stepping quietly on dolomite floors to their paneled office suites will *never* permit reading to revive. The battle is not only one between reading and images; it is a battle over the hearts and minds of vulnerable youth. Interestingly, corporate executives at the highest levels are the only persons on the planet so rich they don't have to know how to use a computer.

Yet is it impossible, somewhere, somehow, to imagine a public school system in America which would employ something like the Pearson model in the early years, where it especially belongs, and then, in a refined progression, creatively supply — in the humanities in particular — the facts, dates and "means" which must also accompany a poetic approach? Would it not be possible, then, to objectively test specific knowledge to ensure competency without ever losing the delight and wonder which properly underlie true lifelong learning? Why would it not be possible to develop the memories of elementary students to impressive degrees, and then add into such a process the study of Latin or another language (Spanish is now the obvious choice), eventually supplementing it with complete, systematic grammatical understanding? Why a second, or even (as in Europe) a third language is not taught in the elementary grades, when the brain is hardwired to learn it, simply boggles the mind. Most language studies in America begin at 13 or 14 — exactly when the mind's neural circuitry begins to shut down language acquisition.

In this process of fixing American education, the teacher, not the student, should be the first target. Salaries should be significantly raised, and at the same moment, only the brightest, most enthusiastic teachers — with actual subject degrees — be allowed into the classroom. The education degree must be entirely abolished. Enhanced salaries, improved social status and high demands on teachers will act, over time, to make the teacher an object of respect and veneration as he or she is in the Orient, or in Germany or in France and other highly developed countries. We do not value teachers, because we do not value education. We would have fixed it by now if we did. This is another way of saying we do not value children — a fact pretty hard to dispute with a 60 percent divorce rate and our continuing casual attitude toward abortion.

These changes do not require outrageous sums of money, nor the addition of a single computer to a classroom. Any nation which can shell out on a moment's notice over $200 billion to cover the tails of the greedy perpetrators of a savings and loan scandal, so that they can continue to play golf on Hilton Head, can fix education in this country. It's a matter of vision and commitment: If every other developed democracy is able to impart basic knowledge to its children, who then demonstrate it every year by whuppin' us in every imaginable test category, why can't we do the same?

Indeed, a nation which destroys the vital categories; which casts doubt upon the True, the Good and the Beautiful; which submits to the easy lie of relativism with unquestioned faith, discarding common sense in the process, is sure to lose its educational bearings, for the very means by which they can be defended begin to erode at the root. The end of liberal education was never merely to acquire a job skill or a pass into the professions. It was, or should be, to ascertain the role of one's vocation in a full and reasoned life, part of a lifelong process of educational unfolding which does not stop with the degree. The idea of the construction worker or the machinist reading Plato in the evenings is the most democratic, and therefore most American and patriotic, of images. How quaint all of this may sound — until you've experienced it.

In the end, we must sympathize with, not condemn, teachers today at the primary and secondary level. Often, too often, they are asked unreasonably to pick up the pieces of a society few would call coherent—fragmented, as we are, to our shame, by drugs, unprincipled violence, a runaway oligarchy controlling the means of production, and a whole slew of unimaginable surrenders from disappointing political frauds to teen pregnancy, killer epidemics to divorce (the latter being among the worst excesses of our time in its savage impact on children). It is a wonder our children are performing at all, given a cultural disintegration already very far advanced; or that teachers still consent to teach for low pay, low status, guided by administrators whom no one would identify as scholars. The wonder of present American education—in the face of the talk shows, the ubiquitous Disney stores, the triumph of Clinique moisturizers over everything else—*is that it functions at all.*

While education may need improving, I am particularly condemning the rough beast, its hour come round at last, which our "culture"—by no means a civilization in the true, high sense—has become; each part so cunningly compromised that even to say *there* is where we must begin to fix it all is well nigh impossible. Even for an agnostic like myself, Eliot's comment in *Choruses from the Rock* rings true: we are the first civilization, Eliot says, ever to give up one God, not for another God, but for no God. Such a virus was predicted by all the great poets and artists in the beginning years of the century, as if the symbolic disintegration of World War I were not enough. Along the way, the process of scientizing the humanities began in the great universities. Schools of severe skepticism arose there and were rewarded at the highest academic levels.

That process in philosophy had telling results. Ludwig Wittgenstein's vow that he would wreck philosophy once and for all and reduce it to grammatical relations among bounded symbols—which he did (by destroying any necessary connection in human languages between the sign and the thing signified)—has resulted in philosophy's nearly complete moral irrelevance to our society today. Its silence is far more execrable than God's. It is an unconscionable betrayal of philosophy's charge to speak directly to the Inner City, and reach its youth with a message of hope or endurance, or kill itself trying. Where *are* the philosophers? When I was growing up at least there was Eric Hoffer. I remember, as a child, actually seeing Hoffer on *The Tonight Show*. All that is left of a "popular philosopher" in the present day is the aging Mortimer Adler — utterly unknown to the man in the street, dismissed by his fellows in the academy as a buffoon for trying to make philosophy relevant to the "common" man (the single most damning denigration possible in academe). The Pearson professors were similarly dismissed and, finally, forcibly silenced, as we have seen. Philosophy, having made itself irrelevant, its professors content to enjoy the unbounded fruits of tenure without accountability to a society they have a moral responsibility to help lead, is fast approaching Classics as the smallest suite of offices in the building

The discipline's other dubious contribution to the twentieth century's cultural life was, of course, existentialism, whose basis lay in an exquisite, almost precious, elaboration of the self, enthroning the concept of choice as the surest route to individual being, and throwing in the absurd concept of the *acte gratuit* along the way as an assertion of radical freedom. Since existentialism is atheistic at its core, it's not surprising that Camus should have seen the concept of self-annihilation (not a middle class option for most of us) as the one supreme philosophical question. And there we go again: the most obvious problems of the twentieth century, crying out for address and redress, have not been problems relating to the *self* but to *society*. Hitler, Stalin and Mao (and all their other sub-simian luminaries from Tito to Benito) constituted the most enormous of challenges for our time — and philosophy, instead, whiled away the hours by going *inward*. A philosophy that can provide no coherent critique of ethics is useless before totalitarianism, and will, in fact, be used by it, first to seize power and then to sustain it. Within the humanities, philosophy has most let down our troubled age. Just as architecture produced individual buildings of significance without being able to withstand the rapacious developers who wrecked the landscapes in which they were dropped, philosophy offered no coherent defense (I mean particularly the American universities) against totalitarianism even as it spread its suffering everywhere. How could it? By its own admission, an entrenched skepticism had silenced it.

Even Einstein's theory of relativity — a specific theory in the physical sciences mathematically representing the relationship between space and time, having no bearing whatever on any of those ethical precepts which govern a society — was somehow taken over in the new *zeitgeist* as a validation of the relativity of values. But the results of science (as distinct from its practice, which is highly value-laden) never tell us anything about the human moral condition, particularly results in physics. Such distinctions are now lost in the mist, of course. Very nearly everybody believes, or behaves as if they believe, that "everything's relative," that there can be no set of truths in the moral sphere which are true for all times, peoples and places.

Writing in *The Opening of the American Mind*, Mortimer Adler recounts how simple Socratic arguments proving the universality of moral truths by logical means are often dismissed as mere word play or intellectually non-binding word-magic — even by his university peers. Our faith in our own powers of logic is so far gone, now, to say nothing of simple common sense as it bears on profound, though simple, moral issues, that even educators cannot grasp them and retreat into caution. Now, of course, if one accepts that there is no connection between signifiers, concepts and objects that would permit you to say, "Stealing my wallet is wrong," let alone "Gimme that back or I'll take your arm off" — if, as Wittgenstein concluded, *all* questions of morality and ethics are philosophically impermissible — I guess I'm never gonna get my money back, nor will the West its senses.

The fact that no one could care less about what Wittgenstein said may be because no one lives in such a loopy universe to begin with (including whole societies founded on jurisprudence, or those professors who vie like corrupt county politicians to get into the journals to publish in his name); and also because Wittgenstein served in the Hospital Corps in World War I for, as he admitted, "moral" reasons. He was a genius of a logician, no doubt about it (as Bertrand Russell attested), and a splendid modern sophist as well — a man who said he believed one thing and did another. *That's* the kind of message to warm the cockles of a good fascist dictator's heart.

The skepticism which the professionalization of philosophy

produced, downwind from the seminal influence of Wittgenstein and the logical positivists, is shared now by the rest of the humanities, whose many current schools (jargon-filled as they are) all amount to one large restatement of relativism which does nothing to encourage, instruct or delight idealistic youth embarking upon a college career. These currents, as in philosophy, do wonders for the publish-or-perish graduate machine, however, part and parcel of the grab for tenure which young professors are forced to make if they are ever to be more than adjunct professors tending bar. Many voices decry the "graduate system" as perverse, but everybody participates in it, and it is, at this moment, as virulent as ever due to the flood of young Ph.D.s seeking jobs, especially in the humanities. It has prompted one of the all-time oddest swerves in educational history: the vehement reinscription of the university as a research factory whose professors, even in the humanities, are rewarded, not for teaching, but for publication and research. An odd use of taxpayer money, especially when parents trustingly assume their children are going to college to be taught by professors whose principal focus is the classroom.

In the domain of literary criticism, deconstruction enjoys a current vogue in America — a school which, building upon the proved imprecision of language, discovers subtle contradictions within the "text," revelatory of contradictions within the intentions of the author. Then, in a comical displacement of the author, the newly valorized critic (as a so-called "imperial reader") then "deconstructs" the text to reveal its actual meaning, which turns out to be nothing. It can't be anything because any underpinnings of meaning have been cut out from under the text by the deconstructive process. Brain surgery for Kipling.

Two corollaries follow. The author's misguided assumptions were not an ascent to truth (as that dumb ol' author, Shakespeare, thought), but merely a revelation of his or her race, class, economic status and gender. This person Shakespeare didn't really write *King Lear*, in other words; the economic conditions of mercantile England under Elizabeth, combined with the politics of the court around her, along with authorial associations about English primogeniture and changing family structures, as well as the advent of new geographic discoveries, filtered through the brain of an *arriviste* male actor who parted his hair to the left, wrote *King Lear*. The deconstructionist, in short, edifies Shakespeare. Shakespeare doesn't edify him.

I have never encountered such an arrogant inversion of critical propriety by a bunch of intellectual pygmies as this, and, as history throws them all, one day, into the trash heap, future ages will marvel that educated people could have wasted so many college loan applications on such endeavors. What could a young person, who deserves something from his professors — some shred of guidance, good counsel, or truth — take away from a school of literary thought that *hates literature?* The professor who espouses such absurdities at the top of the intellectual ladder bears a far greater guilt than does the "lowly" schoolteacher I chided for not reading enough. These professors *really* "teach, but can't do."

Secondly, the deconstructionists not only denigrate the author: They denigrate the poor *reader* too! The thinking is that *the act of enjoyment of the book* is itself — as with the author who wrote it — merely the confession (indeed cannot be otherwise) of the reader's race, class, economic status and gender. The act of reading is made as suspect as the veracity of the text. Enjoyment is, like the text, merely an "artifact" of one's cultural conditioning, in which we are always straitjacketed and above which we cannot rise. The entire concept of universality in literature, and of the kinds of distinctions between works which make up the traditional canon, disappear. In one fell swoop, both truth and the pleasure (no, even the *possibility*) of self-improvement are gone.

Why read at all, then? And of course, that's exactly where I've been heading: At a time when America's only educational future lies in reading — participatory, innocently idealistic reading of the type I encountered in the Pearson Program — the university is perversely undermining reading *as a concept* at its root. In the process it has created a whole class of chichi new superstar critics in gold chains and bad Armani suits, strutting and fretting their hour upon the stage, courted and fawned upon by the big academic presses. Nobody's told them that deconstruction was pronounced dead in France, where it all got started, 20 years ago— or that their graduate students' pronunciation of "parole" with a Missouri accent would make a French waiter guffaw.

Deconstruction and its offshoots are precisely what one would expect to happen when — as Frank Nelick wrote — poetry is viewed as being about *words* and not *things;* when it passes out of the realm of experience and remains locked on the page, or the words are merely manipulated among themselves endlessly, until they can mean anything. It is telling that deconstructionists frequently declare "nothing exists outside of the text." Yet the poem, as most poets will tell you, was never meant to be locked hermetically on the page, or recycled like paper products, but is, rather, to be carried out into the physical world of experience, endowing that experience with numinous rarity. This is what I meant when, echoing the words of the poet James Dickey, I noted that poetry makes possible the most personal kind of possession of the world. Nobody ever thought language wasn't imprecise. Nobody ever thought a poet, like anybody else, doesn't harbor internal illusions about his or her own motivations or place in the world. Nor did anybody ever think that one's place in the world wasn't shaped by a degree of social conditioning, one's view of sex or one's economic status. But dear God, to elevate these commonplaces to the level of inflexible critical laws would be merely laughable if it wasn't, in actuality, having such a profound effect on gullible students.

Every graduate student I knew when I got my master's in English was into this. It was absolutely understood that to gain our professor's approval we had to line up behind one or another of these arcane, jargon-laden theoretical approaches. When Fredric Jameson, a Marxist "superstar" from Duke, visited our classroom one day I was appalled at his visceral, instinctive condescension and arrogance. He chalked up a list of the major critical schools on the board and said, "Choose." The choice, he implied, would essentially dictate everything that would follow in one's thinking about written works, delimiting literature in the process. Fresh from the Pearson Program, I could spot a sophist when I saw one — and indeed I never loathed a teacher for his insolence more in all my time in the classroom, except once: a philosophy professor from Harvard, a specialist on Kant, who would pay students to give him cigarettes to smoke in class.

Ideas turn out to have tremendous force. And here is the great problem with such species of relativism, whether they are dressed up on the spines of books of big name academic presses, or those on display at the mall: Relativism opens the door to fascism. It cannot provide a moral defense against it. And it does, therefore, assist it by passive means. Again and again in this book I have come back to the social and moral order, the fabric of our lives, the texture of our society, because I am, in the end, fiercely patriotic, fiercely democratic, and I believe the way lies open for a decline (quite possibly due to some general economic collapse) for precisely such fascistic elements to reappear on the world scene, possibly here, when at the moment we do not believe such a thing is possible. History is replete with examples of sudden irruptions of barbarity, where, a few years before, everything seemed serene. Why not just stick to this century? Charles Griswold noted of deconstruction, in the pages of *The New York Review of Books*, "Nothing in deconstruction provides an ethical criticism of Nazism.... [It] dissolves notions of personal accountability and responsibility.... [Indeed deconstruction] ... renders theoretically unintelligible basic moral terms such as good and evil." The truth, as Dinesh D'Souza also points out, is that "nothing in deconstruction *permits* such a criticism [of Nazism]."

We have thus seen that the professionalization of philosophy, which undermined truth, has been matched by the professionalization of literary studies, which undermined meaning. Specifically, deconstruction has struck at the heart of literature itself, by destroying the meaningfulness of reading as a personal and undying good. At the very moment the young are immersed in an ever-growing media environment which is manifestly hostile to reading — and which seeks constantly, and successfully, to supplant it with images — the academy has done its little bit to help slit reading's throat. The perversity of the present academy can hardly be overstated in its continuing defense of such ideas. Although any critical views deserve open and honest debate — indeed this is one of the principal functions of any university — the fact remains that such views are now dominant, and will only become more dominant as a significant percentage of older, "traditional" professors begin retiring in the years just ahead. Inevitably they will be replaced by young bloods so overspecialized, or so intent upon the promotion of a school of critical thought (often with an explicit political agenda attached) that they will succeed in burying the stabilizing influence of traditional concepts of the canon once and for all. English studies will become cultural studies. Censorship in the name of political correctness is already well underway. How ironic that it came from the left, not the right.

Thus, a new form of university culture is coming into being in the wake of the death of the canon, and critical assumptions — at least in the humanities — which are not simply skeptical of the aesthetic and personal approach to reading, but are actually hostile to it, have gained widespread credibility. With the break-up of the credibility of the canon under these forces, the "traditional" grounding around which fruitful debate of new ideas could occur has come to an end. "There is no knowledge, no standard, no choice that is objective," says Barbara Herrnstein Smith, past president of the Modern Language Association.

Society is humanity's sole protection against barbarity, which is the natural in us. Overcoming nature is a perilous, all-too-frequently unsuccessful process of acculturation and socialization because it requires an over-determination of the rational. The elaboration of the mind is an exercise in epistemology, in education — and of all political systems democracy requires an informed electorate, an electorate determined to participate in the collective decisions of its own governance; indeed, an electorate that sees such participation as a duty required by the ancient concept of the *polis*, however improbably our large urban centers may compare with those of ancient Greece. Experience teaches that the denigration of these values naturally imperils them; neglect of them can imperil the society. Education thus plays a key role in value formation, and it should be apparent that the kind of education I have been advocating has an ethical component, expressed not simply in the person of the teacher, but in what he or she embodies: the love of the truth, and all those things which flow from it. Such an education is also grounded in experience, in which the fruits of the mind — particularly memory — meet and transform the commonplace into the numinous. Finally, true knowledge permits the discernment required to put in perspective the baleful influences all around us or identify solutions out of the welter of difficulties which plague us.

I have said that education, based on the Pearson model — or a just appreciation of poetry and the other liberal arts — permits a kind of possession of the world. I call this the "personalization of meaning," but I realize that to identify it merely is insufficient to explain it, or its transformative power. It begins as a function of memory, proceeds to a process of naming and ends with a deep identification with experience.

The process of identification soon becomes automatic, revealing not only the world to ourselves, but ourselves to ourselves. When I am in my car, snaking up the highway in an unbearable commute, or watching as other cars whiz past me, intent upon strivings we all must make to seek advantage, memory summons up for me — unconsciously, almost unbidden — Eliot's line in "Prufrock" about the street, how everyone there is "impatient to assume the world." But what world? And should we ever want to assume our cast-out state, exiled from the Garden? Isn't Eliot right when he says that our suburban legacy will be only "a ribbon of highway and a thousand lost golf balls"?

Or even at work, at the end of the day, at Eliot's "violet hour, when the eyes and back turn upward from the desk, when the human engine waits, like a taxi, throbbing waiting" some haunting brokenness lies in wait for me. Contrast this sadness with *The Waste Land's* evocation of past splendor, "where the walls of Magnus Martyr hold, inexplicable splendor of Ionian white and gold." Here, you see, is lostness that is me, the inevitable beginning also of the flame of love for others if I am ever to have it, who share this general condition with me. Our broken world: "Falling towers. Jerusalem, Athens, Alexandria, Vienna, London. Unreal."

I have noted that poetry can be an abyss, a sheer cliff of fall, refining and making exquisite the unbearable. Not so that it might be born, but that it might be named. So that when my parents confronted me on October 17, 1986, with news that my fiancée Barbara Erickson had died suddenly of bulimia in Ashland, Oregon, I knew that there was only one possible text equal to the unacceptable, unspeakable news. With that strange, invincible imperiousness I always had with my parents, I motioned them to sit down, and, tears staining my cheeks, went to the library there in our Seattle home. I read out to them then, from my copy of the *Pelican Shakespeare*, the entire final act of *King Lear*, in which the great King carries the body of his beloved daughter onstage, questions the possibility that she could be gone, and dies himself of a broken heart. The numbers of Shakespeare's most fearful work — in which the great chain of being finally snaps — recounted my own bewilderment, which I have never lost; his attempt to encompass and reconcile the unendurable:

> This feather stirs; she lives. If it be so
> It is a chance which does redeem all sorrows
> That ever I have felt.

> I killed the slave that was a-hanging thee.

> I'll see that straight.

> And my poor fool is hanged: no, no, no life?
> Why should a dog, a horse, a rat have life,
> And thou no breath at all?

> Thou'llt come no more.

> Pray you undo this button. Thank you sir.

It was a moment, quite outside of time, in which I was certain art could never more perfectly coincide with life. I was wrong even on this score. Two hours after Barbara's funeral in Beloit, Wisconsin, her father died, literally, of a broken heart, suddenly collapsing in the garage from a massive heart attack. As I watched and heard Lester Erickson die not six feet away from me, I knew that the end of poetry is to discard it and assume the full weight of unvarnished, unmitigated reality. The sometimes harshness of these pages partakes of that ferocity, that promise to myself: *I killed the slave that was a-hanging thee!*

The personalization of meaning permits the most direct manner of identification with the world. The tools it uses to permit this identification *are* the humanities, and they are the province of every life, obtainable (in libraries if nowhere else) if we truly desire them.

But the humanities permit us to see into *solutions* to cultural problems as well.

The central message of this book is the following insight, and I have put it in capitals so that no reader can miss it: THE SOLUTION TO THE "PROBLEM" OF TECHNOLOGY IS, PRECISELY, A LIBERAL EDUCATION. A liberal education places technology where it belongs — as a tool (and a very useful one) — because a good liberal education elaborates a clear system of values and places what is important ahead of what is utilitarian. Technology is first, always, properly and yet merely, a means to an end, and a liberal education teaches exactly what those ends are. I have suggested as a corollary to this that technology must not be allowed to subvert every aspect of the profession, even as we strive to integrate it wisely into a library context, nor erode the very values of education we are put here to serve. We must always bear in mind that the future of libraries is not technology, though lately we have been tempted to think so. The future of libraries is people.

Technology — especially its recent manifestations, from television to the Internet — will degrade a mind not sufficiently versed in a hierarchy of knowing sufficient to subdue it. This is why education is the key to its control, and why I have treated education, and the humanities in particular, at such length. I have signaled a concern for American education, a concern shared by nearly everybody, because its erosion opens the way for technology's increasing dominance of children's lives, only one among many baleful forces. The humanities are the shortest route to effectively assigning technology its proper role, not only in our lives and those of our young people, but in those priorities which we would yet assign to the postmodern library.

Chapter 4

Whither the Postmodern Library?

The postmodern library, from which I write, is a mirror held up to the postmodern world. That world, at every level, rocks gently now in a bath of ironies too numerous and subtle to count, and, of course, partakes of those very human delusions which have characterized the toolmaking animal since he first dropped from the trees onto the African savannas some three million years ago, and created — against all odds — the whole of human history.

One characteristic of twentieth century man, besides a vague sense of unease (which is about to get *much* stronger), has been his inability to martial enough wisdom to prevent civilization, which is a very fragile thing indeed (a subtle confluence of art, culture, economics and politics) from being eroded, shaped and raped by technology. New tools come into being innocently enough by arguably the most successful human institution ever created: science. But there is no evidence that current societies — or individuals — were bequeathed by either natural or previous cultural evolution the ability to sustain the exponential rates of change we are now experiencing, and of which the postmodern library is a part. "You will only find the bits and cry out because they were yourself," the eminent anthropologist Loren Eiseley has written, plaintively. This may well become the epitaph for our singular age. And if the Book falls, as I am now convinced it will, it will become the epitaph for libraries.

This book is essentially piacular, mourning the loss of one historical form of librarianship, which I have identified with the sacred, for another that is barely even secular; a loss which is already accomplished, and over which it would be pointless to quarrel. It would be still more pointless to attempt to click the metaphysical mouse on <return> and try to "return" librarians and librarianship to the past: its "inner-finishedness," to use a term first coined by Oswald Spengler in his *Decline of the West*, was inevitable from the moment a clerk in the Ohio College Library Center in Dublin transmitted the first cataloging record out into what then passed for cyberspace. The German title for *The Decline of the West*, an equally piacular work, can be literally translated, "The Down-going of the Evening Lands."

If I have taken the license of mourning the inevitable in these pages it is because I grew up loving and using the traditional library, loving its silences, stacks, dust and chambers for reading, and because almost no librarian I've talked to misses this library today. In library school, over a decade ago, the wonders of the new information technologies were already being pressed upon all of us. My professors' view, which embarrassed me a little, coincided with their concept of librarians as captains of a brave new information revolution. I felt even then that knowledge and scholarship — the only true goals I could imagine for any educational enterprise — were being undermined. And so they have been. History, which has always ignored us, will end now by condemning us. We cannot hide from our most insightful patrons the denigration of values which has invaded our walls and made us the marionettes of big business.

Perhaps these themes are immediate to me because I live where the United States ends; beyond this border, poverty, corruption and suffering are written across the heart of a whole continent. The unspeakable sums we spend on technology are unknown in the world beyond our borders. Survival, naked and naïve, is their citizens' only imperative. As these continents and subcontinents disintegrate, as they must, in the coming decades, it will increasingly erode the previous isolationist integrity of the United States and Europe. Our neat projections for ongoing, uninterrupted flows of happiness — which we have imagined is our "right" no matter how poor our neighbor — are about to be downsized. Anyone who cannot see this must be clinically blind. Thus, utopianistic visions of any kind, whether of government officials in Washington D.C. or library professors in Washington state, make me very skeptical indeed, especially about hastily abandoning traditional forms and assumptions in place for hundreds, if not thousands, of years. When the bubble of unprecedented security we've managed to enjoy since 1945 finally breaks, all that will matter after the screams have abated is that we stood for the right things.

Call him Felipe. He is an emanation from that vast brokenness to the south, a brokenness impossible to heal and for which there is no comfort. His perseverance is all the more amazing because it is largely good-humored. I cannot say when he first came to me at the reference desk to try to stump me. 1991? 1993? He would ask me to spell difficult words. He would solicit large reference books from me on organic chemistry. Felipe piled up multiple volumes of encyclopedias of music history in his carrel, to my delight and to the annoyance of the circulation staff. He was not a student, never created a disturbance, and had an almost European sense of manners and decorum for which I could not account — all this despite living in a corrugated cardboard box somewhere down by one of the international bridges. His development of complex theories of musical notation led him to write a book over 800 pages long. I helped him obtain information on copyrighting it, and in fact he did so, although the money for postage to Washington D.C. was difficult for him to obtain. Later, Felipe developed — as the wounded homeless sometimes do — an elaborate conviction (which he researched for 15 hours a day) that the cleaning agents at the college were making him, and everybody else, sick. What was remarkable was the persistence he brought to his research. When I read his prose, I noted that he wrote at a level far beyond most of our students; and as we fell more and more often into conversation I was also surprised to learn that he had studied the flute at the Chicago Conservatory at some time in the remote past and occasionally played in our college symphony. When Felipe would disappear, sometimes for several weeks, the staff and I would fret over his whereabouts. This is a rough town for anyone on his own, especially anyone on the streets. On a few occasions I made sure he had breakfast at the student union. One winter, noticing that his shoes were all but gone, I bought him some cheap Nikes — a gesture he never forgot.

Things changed recently when we brought up our Internets. Once Felipe discovered the Net — and especially e-mail — he became instantly addicted, just like everybody else. The mesmerizing nature of the medium overwhelmed him and any sense of manners. And, regrettably, for the first time he became a problem to us — refusing to end his searching when his time limit was up, forcing me to kick him off with increasing bluntness. Complaints began coming in. Felipe's use of reference books — like our conversations on politics, music, and art — also ceased, and his literary efforts foundered. He wrote 25-page letters on e-mail to Japanese radio stations for reasons no one could ever discover. The humane component of our friendship came apart for good, simply because he never looked up anymore. This medium, like television, grounds its enthusiasts in an eerie isolation — and it's nothing like the gentle isolation of reading a book; there's nothing leisurely about it. It obviously resembles the etiology, not of education, but addiction. I am hardly the first person to have discerned this.

And so it has been with our students, as I have noted. Because the Internet, like television, really *is* the message. The medium becomes the end itself, even though, in the case of the Internet, those doing actual research are usually combing unassisted through thousands, sometimes millions, of websites, most of which are, frankly, junk. Of course if they ask me, I can — through the simplest of Boolean search techniques — pare those searches down to a useful set in seconds. But that's the point, isn't it? They *don't* ask. Because they don't look up. How can their use of the library, then, as an educational experience, be anything other than compromised? And how can reference librarians hope to ever have the quality of contact we once had with our patrons? There is nothing to do about this, of course. I am simply stating a fact we librarians had a hand in cementing into place, and citing it as an example of one of the ironies to which I alluded at the beginning of this chapter. *The postmodern library always deconstructs itself.*

Only, as I have noted, when I encounter students in the reference stacks do my interactions with them instantly become meaningful. Which leads me to restate the obvious: We have invented the library as waystation. Watched the emptying-out of the reference interview. Tolerated the consequent devaluation of the role of the librarian himself. And ignored the alienation of older patrons who would rather flee than use a computer. We've also subverted budgets for traditional materials to pay for the expensive workstations, which never sleep and which are costly to maintain. Librarianship is walking a risky line indeed in embracing its new version of itself. No public debate occurred a decade ago when these steps were initiated; the new library, from the patrons' point of view, just appeared overnight with the sudden, incredible loss of the card catalog. No one within the profession paid attention to those few dissenting voices in our midst who pointed out that — just perhaps — concurrent catalogs (paper and online) be kept to ease the transition for the computer-shy, as a hedge against still unproven and nascent online systems or the inevitable crashes that would occur.

It was that arrogance which drove Nicholson Baker and Sally Tisdale into public print in the nation's leading periodicals. And to them we have offered no effective response, either in our own journals or, especially, in the mainstream press. Why? Their arguments for measured change and transition, from the thinking public's point of view, are well nigh irrefutable. But they contradict the intentions of the administrators, who have rammed change down everyone's throat. We have avoided all along the possibility that there is an indefinable *spiritual* component to what we do and to what has been lost. No one ever said that libraries shouldn't incorporate new technologies. What we should be decrying is their thoughtless conversion from a paradigm based on knowledge to one based wholly on information.

The only truly important cautionary work to have emerged is Michael Gorman and Walt Crawford's *Future Libraries*, which is an excellent monograph and which speaks effectively to this issue. Yet I do not think it goes nearly far enough in gauging how imperiled the library's entire future is relative to technology, nor in placing the postmodern library where it presently is: afloat on the sea of American meaninglessness in which information first seduced, and then eviscerated, knowledge, from infomercials to C-Span. Of course the

McLibrary did not invent this dilemma, it merely lent a helping hand. And the hand that we reached out to join with was — whose? — big business. When in the past did we ever want to sleep with *them?*

OCLC, at least, is nonprofit, was born within the profession and is therefore fairly respectable when it comes to the public or academic nature of our calling (even if its annual reports are getting slicker every year). But with the advent of big-time, for-profit automation vendors purveying large integrated systems, libraries finally took the last, fateful step into sleeping with American late-phase capitalism. And there's one thing you can always count on with a corporation: They'll do absolutely anything to help you out of your money. In our own library, our vendor has the warm, understanding heart of a Mako shark, and if the folks there can stick it to us they always do. Now of course, it's nothing personal. And that's the point. That's been the point of this entire book. Libraries, once sucked in by the vendors (boy were they glad, at first, to test their products on us! We must have looked as gullible as Ellie May or Jethro whittlin' on the porch) now have to suck up to them if anything not in the contract goes awry. And when trouble comes, it's always nice to have an 800 number to call so you can instantly get an answering machine 24 hours a day.

How flattered we were, indeed, when an out-of-control egomaniac like Bill Gates flung us, like deer corn, a few thousand computers — a sum amounting to a laughable pittance of his total wealth — so that *Library Journal* could, like a trained puppy, sit up, bark and put him on the front cover of the magazine for "Wiring the Library" with his own computers. He even schnookered his way onto the ALA Council, despite the ludicrously obvious nature of the ploy. Something tells me, though, that nobody on the council's got a chance of being invited to cocktails at his Mercer Island compound outside Seattle. Too bad. I'm told it has quite a view.

Let me be blunt about this: I hate big business. I hate late-phase, unregulated capitalism, because it created all the strip malls and all the tinker-toys that our young people (the students I'm charged to work with) are being manipulated into wanting, in order to make people like Bill Gates and Roy Disney absurdly rich. And these same people have now invaded the library with a vengeance, with their understated suits and their terrific haircuts, and unstated contempt for anything that isn't a column with a total at the bottom. They've got a hook in us now, and from now on, in varying degrees, and in one form or another, we will be driven by their demands. Compared to their corporate fellows who live this game, we must have seemed easy pickings indeed. A little flattery and a slideshow can go a long way with people used to feeling marginal, either on campus or in the city's budget. They sold us on speed, self-directedness and "efficiency"—that above all—and yet absolutely nothing in education is served by any of these values. In fact they're antithetical to education. And in the end, they're antithetical to reading. And it is in the singularly personal act of reading, as I have said, that any rebirth in an educational system as wigged out as ours must begin.

Recently I took a tour of one of the new postmodern libraries, in which, appearances to the contrary, something was seriously askew in the Land of Oz. The postmodern library adapts well to the theories behind postmodern architecture: Traditional forms may be borrowed from the past, mixed up without rational connection, and thus become masks or facades without any "content" behind them. Postmodern buildings mirror, therefore—in this most cynical of architectural movements—the contextless society in which they are dropped. There are no objective "ideals" for architecture to aim at, because all ideals are "socially constructed" and therefore inherently relative.

In the case of the library I visited, as part of a group, these notions seemed well played out. Technology had sodomized any sensible regard for book or periodical collecting and thus denigrated the very concept of reading. Even the layout of the building worked against it.

After we descended from the bus, we were met at the tinted glass doors of the gleaming new edifice by one of the library staff who ushered us into an enormous "community room" with 20-foot high ceilings. Along the left wall ran an incongruous array of chafing dishes. Our lunch, we wondered? Adjoining these were tables covered with tablecloths and arrangements of plastic flowers. Eventually other librarians from the region began to arrive, and about a quarter of the immense room filled up. I have no idea how much stack space such an immense room might have amounted to.

Then the director, a fierce, plump woman — no doubt embedded in the minutiae of city politics — welcomed us all ceremoniously and, after introducing the staff, announced that one of them, a young mustachioed man, would demonstrate the room's sound equipment. The young man waved from the glass enclosure of a sound booth at the back of the room. Suddenly, at the touch of unseen buttons, the tall windows on the right side of the room began to be closed by electric panels sliding silently into place, propelled by tiny, whirring electric motors. It was like something out of a James Bond film. Of course, the group whistled like bumpkins at this little touch of theater, but I couldn't help thinking how many books or magazines might have been purchased in place of the little motors.

Our whistles and hoots of approval emboldened the young, mustachioed man to greater feats. Emerging from the sound booth (why, I wondered, would a library, if properly dedicated to silence, have a *sound booth?*), the young man began swinging around what looked like a large Frisbee — another remote control device, of course — and, at the touch of another button a digitized movie began playing on a huge screen which had slid silently into place at the far end of the room. It was then that I saw the speakers, and ducked for cover. Fifteen feet high, they began to rumble with a terrific, frightening bass. An earsplitting soundtrack began. With fiendish delight the young man kept cranking the dial up and up. I simply could not imagine that — despite his shouted assurance that the room was "fully soundproofed" — the music we were hearing was inaudible to people trying to read in the main library.

Later, as I shook my head and patted my hair back into place, the tour proceeded with that kind of carefully plotted cunning by which one is hammered over the head with how spectacular the new edifice you're now in is — and therefore how provincial your own must be. Each new demonstration was of some large, turbo-driven technological wonder. We were shown a CD changer with 200 disks, housed in a small, super-cooled room containing, the group was told, a phenomenal $800,000 worth of high-tech equipment. We were also told, rather unceremoniously, not to touch anything. Everywhere we went, everything was state-of-the-art, the best. It was a postmodern librarian's dream. The historical collection, although there was not a single patron in it at 11:00 in the morning, had rich, dark hardwood cabinets and motorized compact shelving, movable by punch-in computer codes, which, alas, the librarian on duty could not remember how to operate.

After the sound-blaster speaker experience, a visit to the million dollar Frigidaire and its untouchable keyboards and consoles, and the tour of the historical collection with its beautiful, immovable stacks, we moved on to the children's section, where we found kids teeming at the Internet terminals. A single solitary boy in thick glasses wandered the book stacks, which I found, upon examination, to be well stocked with excellent titles. Not a single plump pillow invited a child to sit down and read (or dream or imagine or muse), although a large book nook was available with no one in it.

Of course the Internet mesmerizes children like everyone else, and if given a choice few children will read when the Net is available. It's not only an interactive event for them; it's a group event. I cannot imagine what a steady diet of the Internet does to children when one also adds in the claim television makes on their time. It is one of those ironies that the ALA's much-lauded "Read" posters feature photos of celebrities any kid in America would instantly recognize, holding books by famous authors whose picture no kid in America would ever recognize. So there it was in the library I was touring: the postmodern library deconstructing itself yet again. Internet terminals stupidly introduced into the very area where children are supposed to be reading, thereby guaranteeing that reading will be eroded. And the evidence is right in front of our eyes. I have no idea why a profession continues to make such choices, ignoring the evidence of common sense, the opinions of our most thoughtful and loyal patrons, the remonstrances which have appeared in national periodicals which inform the nation's best minds, the lessons of history, the ethics by which we may claim to be a profession in the first place, and the needs of the democracy we are supposed to be serving.

But strangest, most egregious of all, was the circulating book collection of this most postmodern of libraries. The books were housed (inconveniently) on the second floor — one would think they would be the centerpiece of the collection, but that is reserved for the gleaming computers on the first floor. When the expensive, stainless steel doors of the elevator opened and discharged us I beheld row after row of half-empty shelves. Because I was told that, in the midst of all the budgeting for whirring motors, fancy CD jukeboxes, sound systems, electric screens, mirrored elevators, unprogrammable mahogany coffins, and fake flower arrangements, no one, including the director, had actually asked for any money for more books when the library moved from its old, cramped quarters downtown.

Now this is a library in a city where the written word might turn out to mean something, because many of its citizens are poor, haltingly bilingual, and the only way forward, for them and for their children, must be an intense commitment to reading and self-education. It is almost an afterthought to describe the periodicals collection in this library — if you could call it that: stuck around a corner on the second floor, by a lonesome copier, it occupied an area not much larger than two broom closets placed end-to-end. Thus I was forced to conclude that, except for an excellent collection of children's and reference books (which I personally examined), this library — built at a cost of nearly $10 million, in one of the poorest cities, per capita, in the country — was actually antithetical to reading, the life of the mind and (once I discovered its Internet terminals had blocking software) even the intellectual freedom which every adult is constitutionally guaranteed.

I left the library feeling that every fearful tremor I'd ever had about the present and future state of libraries had at last been enfleshed. Climbing back into the bus with my enthusing colleagues I could not help recalling the lone figure of Spencer Shaw standing forever by the bus stop in the littered street in Seattle, with the air chilling around him and an inhospitable winter coming on. The postmodern library not only deconstructs itself — it insults thinking people.

As it happens, I was not the only one to be insulted, or to notice that something screwy had happened deep in the blueprints of everyone involved in building this anomaly. A letter from a concerned citizen was brought to my attention in the city's local paper decrying the paucity of the new library's books, the prevalence of far too many

computers and the outrageous expense of the building and its appoint-
ments, whose postmodern architecture (bright colors, odd angles, an
absurd, high-cost tower housing nothing more than a staircase) neither conveyed nor inspired in him the reverence or timelessness
befitting a temple of learning. The man, an Hispanic, noted the dis-
service to civic values for minorities which such administrative decisions implicitly represented and the erosion of knowledge they
embodied. When the letter appeared, I waited with bated breath for
the library director's response to such a clear, public challenge.

Nothing. Or, as we say in these parts, *nada.*

A response simply never appeared. It was easier, that is, more cowardly but politically expedient (I guess), to say nothing at all to a citizen who had actually cared enough about libraries and reading to take
the time out of his own busy day to write a letter in good faith, address
it, stamp it, drive to a mailbox and take a conspicuous public stand
than to honor his concern with a shred of corresponding courage. Such
an omission goes beyond neglect of duties, or political expediency, and
shades into insult. Saddest of all, a genuine opportunity had been lost:
for the director to open a sincere dialogue about the tough questions
any library administrator faces. Questions about balancing expendi-
tures for "traditional" sources against vocal patron demands for newer,
ever-more expensive technology; about the role of information versus
the role of knowledge in a library; about spiraling costs here, sinking
budgets there. All this was lost by this particular director's indefensi-
ble evasion. All that remains, in this city, is a "library" playing catch-
up. No scholar, no reader, would ever take it seriously. Stripped of its
trinkets, like its postmodern façade, there is only an infinitely regress-
ing emptiness. Maybe that was the point. Show without substance, just
like everything else. A "socially constructed" space lacking an "ideal,"
empty of meaning, like the mall down the street, where the "products"
(jeans, unguents for the skin, information, Herodotus) cannot be
arranged in a hierarchy because they are all "relative."

The dysfunctional libraries we have managed to create in the last
ten years were not created by average work-a-day reference and catalog librarians, but by top level administrators (mostly male, according to studies) who hate the concept of the old library (symbolized by

the card catalog, which they trashed) and, above all, the stereotype of the dowdy Marian, with her sensible shoes. I owe this insight to Nicholson Baker, who wrote in "Discards":

> The card catalog is to them a monument not to intergenerational intellect but to the idea of the lowly, meek-and-mild public librarian as she exists in the popular mind. The archetype, though they know it to be cheap and false, shames them; they believe that if they are disburdened of all that soiled cardboard, they will be able to define themselves as Brokers of Information and Off-site Hypertextual Retrievalists instead of as shy, bookish people with due-date stamps and wooden drawers to hold the nickel-and-dime overdue fines, their Read-to-Your-Child posters over their heads and February-is-Black-History-Month bookmarks at their fingertips. The proponents of computerization are such upbeat boosters of the library's potential role in the paperless society ... that library managers are encouraged to forget — are eventually frightened even to admit — that their principal job is to keep millions of used books dry and lend them out to people.... [T]he removal of the word "books" from the library's statement of purpose is exactly the act that allows misguided administrators to work out their hostility toward printed history while the rest of us sleep.

I have worked with library directors who have ranged from political geniuses to certifiable imbeciles, and I am convinced that most (though by no means all) fall toward the lower end of the scale. Like administrators everywhere they must be seen to be doing something in the middle tier of a management hierarchy, and this can often lead to forgetting the basic service to which Baker alludes — keeping millions of books dry and then lending them out. With cascading floods of new technology, and now with the advent of distance learning on campuses across the country (another "possibility" that is being reinscribed as a duty, therefore becoming the latest bandwagon), librarians will be busy indeed deconstructing reading for the foreseeable future.

The decline in reading as a value was brought home to me recently as I prepared an exhibit here at our library for National Library Week, as I help to do each year. I decided that a fitting testimony to the values I have been espousing would be a display of the students' responses to a survey I boldly titled "Books That Changed My Life." On the survey form, we asked students to cite three books which had profoundly affected them, one way or another, careful to assure them they "need not be classics," but any books which had influenced them. The responses, what few came in, were disturbing in two ways: First, only one student could even come up with *three* books. This number, for most of them, was apparently too formidable to achieve. Second, and more disturbing, was the quality of the responses. They were, for the most part, monosyllabic — like "learned about history" or "Moby Dick — good book." It was also clear that many of the books had simply been part of recent class assignments. The responses revealed no depth, no *texture* of reflection. And in not a single case did a student cite a book from his or her childhood, as I'd hoped they would. In the end, the exhibit had to be scrapped because the students simply couldn't provide anything to put up on the wall. And it is not because our students are different from undergraduates elsewhere; they are every bit as intelligent as anyone else, and they do seem to be busy. I can only conclude what is obvious to just about every educator I have spoken with, here and in other parts of the country: Young people today develop no profound relationship with books as children, and this simply carries over into college. It hardly seems to matter whether this is due to the disorder caused by an unconscionably high divorce rate, the dumbing-down spawned by the nonstop viewing of television, the rise of unfiltered materialism as the only significant legacy of 1960s, the ignorance of their own teachers who don't read either, or the recent onset of a host of distracting new technologies. The loss of books in the life of most children today is due to all of these things in subtle combinations one could spend a lifetime sorting out.

The frightening point is that if one does not develop such a habit of mind early, it becomes geometrically harder to acquire it later, paralleling language acquisition; and certain reading experiences which are indefinable and mysterious (the dreamy, rapt loss of oneself into a fictional character, like Mr. Toad or Alice or the Velveteen Rabbit) simply cannot be achieved by the adult mind. The consequence is not merely diminishment, as I have repeatedly insisted; it has profound social implications. Children who have not been nurtured on early, profound reading experiences are unlikely to encounter, profoundly, the great texts of the Enlightenment or the Founding Fathers or Greek and Roman history at a later date — and the way lies open, then, for the ethical disintegration of the very society they have blithely assumed would always nurture them, which would always provide an uninterrupted flow of dresses and motorcars and cable channels. Indeed the way lies open for fascism, whether political (God help us) or corporate, which is where we are now, isn't it?

Think for a moment. What would one expect a society to look like, whose tie to the integral Word had been snapped? Why, the one we live in. Young people already accept without protest incredible controls on their lives; they accept without protest that cameras are watching them "for their own safety" in video stores and supermarkets. They accept, as do the rest of us, that to obtain useful employment they must take down their pants for a drug test. Their schools are frequently surrounded by barbed wire, in accordance with the underlying assumption that we cannot trust them. Half the violence in the school may be because we consistently underestimate their actual capabilities, leaving them bored out of their skulls. They are absolutely enamored of the latest styles in clothing, which they purchase in large numbers and at incredible prices, without perceiving that they are being deftly manipulated by huge corporate structures who quietly make sure that new styles emerge each season to satisfy their restless quest for an individual identity — this while, after school, they are glad to join a hamburger corporation in which they are the tiniest, least individual cog and as interchangeable as a sparkplug. All in order to buy the other corporation's jean, leather jacket, sneaker, motorcar, beauty product, CD player, cellular phone or timepiece. Having, like their parents, no sense of history, the intellectual equipment needed to discern how they are being prostituted is unavailable to young people — intellectual equipment which only reading and thinking in uninterrupted silence can provide. And this, too, is exactly what the corporations want.

So, in the end, I wasn't surprised when the students couldn't tell me anything of value they had ever read.

I must confess that this was not the case in my own childhood. I must also hasten to assert that I do not consider myself unusual for having patronized the public libraries of Green Bay, Wisconsin as a boy. I wasn't unusual for being there, though perhaps the imperatives which drove me there were unusual. Many children used the library, as they do today, because their parents were clued into it. In the end, I can only speak out of my own particular experience, which is the following.

I was driven to the library by an undercurrent of inadequacy and fear, and a desire to prove that I could be loved. This strange set of imperatives came about because of the confluence of three singular facts: I had three brothers and no sisters; they were all much older than I, and, at the time, in colleges or universities; and they all were in the process of becoming doctors or surgeons. Each was brilliant or fearfully accomplished, one a magna cum laude, another president of his fraternity, another a track and field star, president of his class, top debater in the state, even prom king. So the list went. Until we moved from Wisconsin in my first year of junior high, I lived with the terrible, frequent reality of constant comparison, such as one school principal's statement, "Oh, Steve's brother? We'll expect great things of you." It could just as easily have been David or Byron.

When I was very young, my mother took me to one of the branches of the Green Bay Public Library, set on a grassy peninsula of land downtown — a building I dimly remember as being of cut gray stone, small but imposing, with high stone stairs. I have thought in the years since that maybe this was a Carnegie library of some kind, perhaps because of its nineteenth century Neo-Gothic severity, which I liked. Inside was Ruth Kuhs, the librarian. She was a member of my father's church, but I think the association I had with her was maternal, because it was my mother who always dropped me off into her safekeeping.

Once, it was the dead of winter and I had been prowling the stacks in Mrs. Kuhs' library. I could not have been much more than five or six. I do not remember anything else about this incident, except the large, blonde-wood library clock — a grandfather clock that was telling the minutes toward closing time at six o'clock. I was curled up in a reading nook with large leaded windows on three sides, books scattered about me, lonely and solitary in the almost-empty building. Mrs.

Kuhs was setting things in order for opening the next day. I remember, since it was already pitch dark, looking out of the windows, which were freezing to the touch. Snow seemingly stretched everywhere — across the great lawn of the library, out into the darkness across the streets, descending in white chips onto the buildings of the city; it fell from the lampposts with their yellow lights, swirling in the gusts of wind from the roofs. The library, and my childish reading, were a dream I was waking from, as six o'clock edged nearer. I remember feeling a sudden, tight little knot of fear take hold of me, because my mother seemed slow in coming, and the world — layered in snow — seemed too large a place. I remember staring at the clock, then: its blonde wood, its white, enameled dial, its old-fashioned hands telling the minutes; but maybe *not* telling them. For I seemed to be unable to awake from the dream — the place, the library, the books, the warm golden light of the empty reading room. Time just stopped. The memory is now embedded in the circuits and neurons of a past I cannot un-remember. And I will always be there, feeling an anxiety, feeling a lostness in the world that the place could not quite overcome, for a child who is in me, who will one day be wiped out, in me. Because, in addition to time, there was one other element: silence. Terribly beautiful, hard, lean, and mathematical, like the gray, fretted stones of the building — severe, but absolutely real. *I loved the silence that made timelessness possible.*

In a few moments, a car honked, I said good-bye to Mrs. Kuhs, and with the open portals of the library backlit behind me, I ran across the crusty snow of the library lawn to join my mother.

Within two or three years, I was developmentally able to feel much more thoroughly the constellation of pressures bearing down upon me by my brothers' growing legacy. The library again became a way of coping with them: I conceived the idea of writing "papers" such as my brothers were writing at Carroll College as a bid for parity — both emotional and intellectual. Touchingly, I had no idea that I was really trying to be loved, offering by this small, child's gesture some incremental pebble to set against the splendid purples and velvet robes and ritual actions of all their unnumbered graduations which seemingly would never, could never, end. No teacher had assigned these "papers" of mine and, indeed, none ever saw them. But I knew they had to involve some component of research — and that meant the library. I had even turned up, in the basement of our home, an old briefcase, discarded by Steve as he made his way through school, which I immediately claimed as a treasure. I abandoned the branch library in favor of the big main library downtown, which shared the building with the Green Bay Museum, presided over by Mr. Quigley, its eccentric curator.

I have no idea today what the reference librarian on duty must have thought when this fourth or fifth grader appeared before him one day, and announced, with briefcase in hand, that he was there to do "research" in order to write "papers." I headed, probably unassisted, out of pride, for the card catalog, and soon found myself in the astronomy section, sitting on the floor and poring over Fred Hoyle's classic *Frontiers of Astronomy,* in which he propounded his famous "Steady State" theory (the theory which was superseded by that of the Big Bang cosmologists just then coming on the scene). I also looked up information on all the planets in the *World Book Encyclopedia,* and began drawing pictures of the planets and the solar system. I learned about light years, lasers, masers, Theodore H. Mainman, basic quantum mechanics and parsecs. What I didn't understand I memorized — enough to give a lecture on ruby lasers, S and P orbitals, photon emissions and flash tubes to my fifth grade classmates, who (I later learned) thought I was both nuts and arrogant.

And I did, finally, write the "papers" I had set out to write on astronomy, and I sent them to my brother Steve. And I visited the museum, frequently, where I remember being fascinated by its many exhibits and dioramas, but especially and unendingly by the coiled green boa constrictor which Mr. Quigley (tall, lean, ironic of humor) had placed in the foyer. On the second floor was a mummy which likewise fascinated me, and which had a terrific tan.

These stories document, for me personally, how deeply embedded the concept of the library can become for people introduced to it at a young age. They also illustrate my devotion to their traditional aspects (silence, reverence, timelessness) which I have been so insistent upon preserving as the foundation of the scholarly life. Finally, they confirm that, in each case, a *person* made a difference: Mrs. Kuhs as a kind of maternal comforter; and, in a related, curatorial capacity, Mr. Quigley as the sharp-witted intellectual. I associated both of them (not realizing it at the time) with reading, preservation, the concept of a discrete collection which is to be curated, that is to say, respected, loved, cared for. These are not bad values to embrace in such a world, and, obviously, they are what led me into the profession.

The writing of this book has been governed largely by experience — what my eyes have witnessed from the vantage point of the reference desk, from the interactions I have had with students and exchanges I have had with fellow librarians in the field. And, when it comes to looking into the future of libraries, I feel certain that a trend, which I first noticed in periodical usage — now well documented by everybody — will eventually claim the book as an entity. The advent of printable articles will doom paper journals and, within a library context at least, most magazines, except those of such a popular nature that they demand browsability in paper form. It is not only the high cost of paper and production which is driving this trend; patrons prefer the "as you need it" convenience of printing articles over the traditional stacks of paper periodicals sitting there "just in case." Online access to full-text, printable articles is truncating the utility of paper periodical collections at lightning speed, and in our library, we like everyone else are already considering cutting journals in paper to avoid duplication.

About the time that I began noticing this trend among our students, our library opened an Internet lab, partly to get all the e-mailers and chat liners out of the building, because they were ruining opportunities in our four walls for serious students to do serious research. As it happens, the new lab is located in a separate building, and, in addition to the Internet, offers the ability to browse the book catalog, access to all of our full-text magazine databases, word processing and spreadsheet software, free printing and, of course, free, unfettered chat and e-mail possibilities.

When the lab was opened, in a large ceremony attended by media personages, dignitaries and college students and staff, no one even found it necessary to mention that it was under the wing of the library. Instead, they talked about the historic nature of the building, which had been charmingly renovated, and which, indeed, used to be the student union in the college's earliest days. A teacher from that time of the college's history spoke at length, and amusingly, of how dances were held in the building, boys met girls, cards were played and newspapers read — how, in short, the whole campus had a kind of center there. And that now it would have a similar place for students to come, this time to interact with students all over the world, if they chose to.

When I visit the lab, since I supervise it, I can go in at 11:00 in the morning, when every one of its 60 terminals is in use, and always be struck by one thing: how unearthly quiet it is except for the incessant clack of the keyboards. I've never seen 60 young people, in close quarters, at 11:00 in the morning, so quiet. Not even in the library. It's *too* quiet. The teacher who spoke at the opening ceremony got it all wrong. There's no interaction here, even though a lounge is available, which is never used, despite comfortable seating. The students' preference is for the lab, where surveys have shown the principal use is e-mail. And though a lab is a different thing indeed from a student union, there is something inhuman about it all. In a desperate move to endow it with something affecting, I put up prints of great master art on the walls, and a series of paintings depicting the college's oldest buildings. Students can go anywhere in the lab along the vagaries of cyberspace, find any fact in recorded human history, ferret out anything that could ever be known. But they never, ever, look at the people sitting next to them. *They could never fall in love.* Like the library, this temple of knowledge is now merely a waystation.

The crucial fact here, however, is that by physically separating the lab from the library itself, large numbers of students who used to come into the library no longer do so; and we have, in a sense, merely become a holding tank for books. In the first two months the lab was open, its usage climbed at a geometric rate — the number of students who use the lab now equal nearly 50 percent of the total weekly head-count of the library during a peak week, and this number will grow. The students in the lab do not have any reference librarians available to them; library assistants, fully trained in computer basics, provide any assistance they might need, but without the subject knowledge of trained professionals. At a time when our library administration is arguing the need for more librarians, the facts would seem to indicate that the students are getting along quite well without us. We made sure of that. If we just siphoned off something like half of our most frequent users — online users who rarely asked for help to begin with — why are *more* librarians needed? Eventually some administrator is going to get wise to this. And there we go again: the postmodern library once again deconstructing itself. The increasing self-sufficiency of users, which may be a detriment to them, and which demonstrably blunts our interactions with them, will soon imperil our jobs. Just as the paper magazine collection is being bypassed for online resources accessed remotely — in a lab, dorm room or at home — I have witnessed the library building (and its librarians) being bypassed, as we become, not captains of the new Information Order they told us we would be in library school, but mere hitchhikers on the Information Superhighway, begging for a ride.

I am just kooky enough to think, for those students who no longer visit us nearly as often, that they have lost something indefinable by not seeing books, handling them, experiencing them — as physical objects — on a daily basis. But what if there shortly will be no books? What if the postmodern library itself, that entity — like its theoretical constructs in literary criticism — deconstructs itself one final time, and forever? I said that if the book falls, then so will we. And I believe this will surely happen, and soon; that in a very short time it will rush upon us like a thief in the night, stealing our last conceivable reason for being. The concept of the *programmable book* is making its way into the public eye — a book-shaped object, with a cover and thin, transparent leaves (200 or 300 of them) which can be "programmed" to give a high-resolution image of a "page"; the device reads exactly like a book, but can be programmed with whole libraries of actual titles. These you will be able to summon up at will. One imagines a period of 20 or 30 years in which every known book on the planet will be feverishly scanned, by mechanical means, into a vast reservoir in cyberspace — and, just like calling up any movie you wish into your television, virtually any title will be available. At that instant of time when the programmable reading unit takes hold, the book — the crumbling, endearing leaves, the tooled bindings, the march of printed words, the end-papers inscribed by the dearly beloved, once, long ago—*will be dead*. And along with it, the concept of the library will have vanished. Its inner-finishedness will be completed. The public library will be an artifact, like the card catalog it discarded, and the virtual library will at last be a reality. The cumbersome book, with which libraries began, was the last thing, finally, which stood in the way of their cultural demise. It is the virtual library which our profession has been driving itself toward obsessively for the past 15 years; it was what we wished for, what our vanity required, what claimed our seemliness — and what we wished for, we are about to receive.

This book, all along, has been about indefinable things. Its insights, all along, have fallen under the domain of poetry and only incidentally under the domain of anything like information science. I have never believed librarianship should be in the sciences, as I told my father there at the window of his last home — just as I have never believed we should be in the vanguard of anything. I treasured all along the very marginality which so many others in the field found an embarrassing stereotype. I endorsed the idea of extreme conservatism toward change as it applies to libraries, at precisely that moment when such an idea was being wholly overthrown. Patience, circumspection, steadfastness; these, I felt were (notice the past tense) the heroic values in a civilization disintegrating into sound bytes. Instead we stood for shallow boosterism, techno-mania, trendspotting, complete lack of historical perspective. The best technology had to offer might have been incorporated into what we do slowly and cautiously, without exploding budgets, disintegrating reference interactions, and imperiling staffing.

Or could it? Finally, here at the end, I must admit the truth: I know very well that revolutions, by definition, cannot be transitional, cannot be controlled, escape efforts to integrate them with the past and always leave behind old ways of thinking without asking our permission or approval. I have said that this book is piacular in nature, a sacred mourning. A programmable book, like a stereo system, like a video deck, can be used to deliver aesthetic experiences, but it cannot be the object of love in itself. It can never bear the trace of passion, inscription, the plea of the loved one to be remembered. At some level, that sacred, indefinite, intangible trace suffused librarianship, emanating from the stacks, inhaled with the motes of dust; stacks which, in their marching, imposing aggregates, were the visible, literal symbol of knowledge for all mankind. The card catalog unlocked their secrets, so that when the card catalog went, when our own imaginative and spiritual dearth as librarians was revealed, the way lay open for all manner of mayhem and desecration. And now the library, as I have said, will fall, *must* fall, its own caretakers either oblivious to what's coming or, to judge from their behavior, eager to help topple it.

Sadly, the loss of the *temenos,* the library's space, the building itself, will, I think, be as profound a loss as anything. The civic benefits of people pursuing knowledge in a public space will be a diminishment to our cities. And another significant symbol of democracy will have vanished — at a time when, as I have indicated, it is being undermined everywhere by a host of baleful forces more dangerous for their subtlety. Things we once could have done only at the library we'll do at home, as we increasingly do already, of course — snug in our gated communities, withdrawn still further behind our alarm systems, surrounded by virtual technologies undreamed of, I suppose. But always further, ever further, from tangibility, from experience. "How does one become Real?" the Velveteen Rabbit asks the Skin Horse. "By being loved," the Skin Horse replies. It is in this way that, first, books, then libraries became real to me. Since an entire epistemological order is ending, such ways of thinking are about to vanish.

I have said that there have been three ages of humanity: oral, narrative, visual. Television really *was* the revolution everyone said it was; it really did have the scale of impact that was predicted for it, and it did create a new world order. And that world order has been almost completely negative. The visual society has been and will always be a disaster for the West — corrupting some of narrative society's most vital achievements, including democracy, education, religion and the family. It fashioned an entire society around itself, extending far beyond the borders of the television screen.

The Internet, and all the other recent technological enhancements which have come our way, *if* controlled, could have been useful to libraries to a degree. But they are not controllable by their very natures. They too are another emanation of Visual Society. And even as we debate their utility, new devices, ever more clever and persuasive, are overwhelming us. They will, I believe, doom libraries altogether. Libraries will not exist in a hundred years. I hope I am wrong, of course, but experience and reason persuade me otherwise. Whither the Postmodern Library? Into the book of time, which silence made possible.

Afterword

The Self That Remains: Recollections of My Father and His Library

"It was the greatest library in Christendom," William said. "Now," he added, "the Antichrist is truly at hand, because no learning will hinder him..."

— Umberto Eco,
The Name of the Rose

I have said that despair gnawed at my father's former certainties in the last years of his life, as if God or the devil had poured a bitter distillment into all the tunnels of his faith. It was, I think, less his own physical suffering — acute though it was — than certain calamities which befell two of his sons; and, more than that, the reflexive operation of literary sensibilities which did not permit him, as it might other people, to reconcile these events. He was too fine a father, and too fine a reader, to accede to the devastating loss of Carol Wisner, my brother Byron's wife, or to the death of my own fiancée. It was not simply the fact of their own unbearably premature endings. My father could see, all too plainly, the roaring, concussing, savage effects on his two sons; sons who would not be comforted. A thorough knowledge of literature, philosophy and the Bible does not act to reassure the fully

111

adult mind: indeed, they will only refine and perfect our apprehension of suffering, endowing it with a poignancy which blocks all evasion. At the very moment when some persons might be looking to others for sympathy, or confessing their brokenness, the literate mind is beginning to step out of the circle. My father began a cycle of quiet dispossession I only imperfectly perceived and could not stop. Love without faith became the hard, stony path up which he labored.

One of my father's favorite authors (he had once visited the University of Salamanca) was Miguel de Unamuno. In his *Tragic Sense of Life* Unamuno wrote, "The man we have to do with is the man of flesh and bone — I, you, reader of mine, the other man yonder, all of us who walk solidly on the earth." I find the memory of my father already fading, against my will — fading before the white noise of middle-class American life; the demands of a mild and blandly respectable professional career and unpossessed aspirations. If I wanted to find my father ("the other man yonder"), where would I look? I cast about and realize that perhaps the "he" I am seeking — the most significant "he" that remains — is to be found not in photographs, not even in the few sermons he apparently overlooked when he thought he had burned them all. I think my father's legacy is to be found most truly in his personal library, which I, as a librarian, inherited after his death. And the meaning of him is both in the books he gave away and the books which remain. If you dispossess one thing you often inherit another, perhaps an even truer version of the truth.

Mine was a childhood peopled by books, haunted by books, shadowed by books. Adamantine convictions grew up around them. Some of the most impressive volumes were kept in my father's study at the red-brick First Presbyterian Church back in Green Bay, Wisconsin.

A friend of mine and I would play covertly around that church's fluted columns — solid Doric constructions, severe, unornamented, accessible only if you climbed up from the street after squeezing past a wrought-iron gate. After running and hiding among the columns with my friend, I would climb back down to the street, go around a corner and ascend the outside stairs that were a back entrance to my father's second-floor study. This ascent to the study was analogous to the two high steps my father climbed every Sunday morning at ten o'clock, when he mounted the pulpit. In retrospect, perhaps climbing the steps also symbolized a thirst for a higher order of language; a language which enthralled both my father and me. Proclamation, exhortation, the hermeneutic of the brimming Word — these were the straps which tightly girded my heart without my realizing it. Strangely, I perceived no irony that the man I talked with so casually over the box of Wheaties at breakfast should be the same man who, just two hours later, stood before me and above me, robed impressively in black robes and padded velvet, speaking about God. Knowing my father as I did, it all seemed perfectly natural.

I have inherited my father's somewhat heavy German features, his prominent nose, the eyes set close together. He was of medium height (I later outgrew him by two inches), and I never saw my father without his horn-rimmed glasses. He never seemed to raise his low, measured voice, even in arguments with my mother. It was, I remember, a deep, theatrical bass perfectly pitched for the sermon form with its latent sense of the dramatic (he reveled in this) and its high seriousness. Oddly, my father's beard stopped at the ear-line; he could never grow sideburns, nor can any of his four sons.

As a child, and especially as a teenager, I raged against his perfectionism, his radical need for precision and his carefully guarded emotional life. Now, as a man intent on preserving certain silences of my own, I admire both his restraint and his severe work ethic — an ethic of achievement and discipline I absorbed that later aided my lonely studies in college. I remember that a B grade on my report cards as a schoolboy always brought a certain brief shadow of disappointment to my father's eyes, which he could not hide entirely, though he tried; to avoid this shame I contrived to make all A's, and usually did.

There were always, it seems, the great questions, which I was feeling for even then. All I knew was that language could frame them, answer them, exhaust them — and that, through skillfully manipulating language, I could disingenuously get the adults around me to move in my direction. I needed vindication. My older brothers' legacy, even at that age, was becoming prodigious and unsettling. The three of them had just embarked on their separate medical and dental careers. My fierce, hopeless longing for them I displaced into books in our family library — books like *The Wind in the Willows* and the famous Hardy Boys mystery series, which I would devour at the rate of one volume per day. I also liked the Tom Swift Science Adventure series, whose presumption of the ascendancy of science and its promise of a better world had captured my imagination.

The Encyclopedia of Animals was also an imposing and well-worn set on our shelves: three hefty, uniform volumes of some seven hundred pages each, bound in durable, light-red canvas; books about virtually every animal in the world, from tarsiers to cobras. Each species was described, along with its Latin name and habitat, in about half a page of text. I would pore over the black and white photographs, grouped in blocks and subdividing each volume of the set. There were numerous line drawings that I liked to study as well.

And another book: *Kildee House*, by Rutherford Montgomery, an author about whom I know nothing. *Kildee House* was a green cloth-bound wonder to me; the story of one Mr. Kildee, who had made his home in the forest against the back of a giant redwood tree — a home he then opened up to all the animals of the forest. He even devised clever, intricate devices and pull-strings to keep cabinets and drawers safely shut from the predations of a mischievous family of raccoons which had taken up residence with him. I had watched raccoons washing pebbles and feeling for crayfish up at our summer cabin in northern Wisconsin, so I knew that Montgomery must have known about them intimately in order to write about them so convincingly.

These books, like another wonderful set we had acquired somewhere — the famous 'All About...' series, which featured dinosaurs, plants, insects, mammals and a host of other topics in the realm of nature — charged my childhood reading with wonder and animation. Do children read like this now? Of course some do; but I suspect ever fewer of these vivid encounters are occurring. Such focus depends on unified parental insistence and vision and possibly on just how much a child needs to read in order to make up for an absence that is palpable and omnipresent, so that filling this absence with language becomes an imperative. Imagination is the key to the precocious child's world of sadness, its butterfly purity and ache. And certainly no genre is so painful for an adult to confront as is children's literature. It conjures a grief-in-recollection which can never be appeased; a primal sadness that is central to the tragic beauty of our separate life-journeys, all those surrenders and excesses that we call growing up.

That such an ache and such a sadness should have unsealed the valves of my childhood attention is a fact which yet another book painfully revealed: *The Wind in the Willows*, by Kenneth Grahame. The story of Ratty, Mole, Mr. Badger and especially — always, famously — Toad, kidnapped my imaginative life with as much force as my vehement rejection of the ridiculous yellow Tonka trucks my mother proffered to me, hoping I would deign to play with them. I never did. Indeed, I come perilously close to adult tears as I attempt to shape here, for the purposes of recollection, the radical meaning I conferred upon Grahame's masterpiece; and as a new father I am already dreading having to read *The Wind in the Willows* to my own growing daughters without the embarrassing betrayal of real tears. It is not that the timbre of the story only became apparent to me later as an adult, after my childhood innocence had been wiped clean by sexuality. No, the mystery of it was that I somehow understood all about the book's autumnal sadness even as an eight-year-old; that I had, even at that age, already reached out and encompassed it from beginning to end. I contrived, perhaps, not to confront too directly those sections which were painful to me (the moving chapter "The Piper at the Gates of Dawn" was among these; also the Wayfaring Rat's temptation to Ratty to visit the "Wide World" beyond the River Bank, finishing with Toad's unbearable conversion and pledge to "be sensible" and give up his grandstanding, which closes the book). Never underestimate the child's heart: neither its capacity for pain, nor its ability to deliberately shunt away from itself the duty to grow up, to "be sensible," to willingly allow Toad and his magnificent flourishes and gestures to perish.

We must acknowledge that every one of these childhood books had a distinct presence of their own. All were hardbound, well-made, heavy and absolute to the touch. I have said that I was posing some very great questions, and it remains true that the physical beauty of the books I was handling as a means of answering these questions was an inescapable part of their meaning. It is unthinkable that a CD-ROM or a portable electronic book could function in such an intimate manner. If I have sounded a cautionary note in these pages against the untoward encroachment of technology on the spaces and forms of meaning, it is precisely because I so much fear its capacity to short-change us by promising false substitutions. But these are heretical thoughts for an aging librarian in the postmodern library's brave new world, with all its amusing, expensive and, I fear, largely unnecessary trinkets.

More seemingly forbidden and less intimate than the fruits of our family library were the books in my father's study at the church. As a child, I did not open these books nor remove them from their shelves. They were vast, multi-volume, adult tomes. My father's massive *Interpreter's Bible* spanned fifteen gray and red volumes and covered every book in the Old and New Testaments. The companion *Interpreter's Bible Dictionary* was a brown and green four-volume set which my father would consult gravely as he was working on his sermon. And then there was an encyclopedia of numerous black volumes from the turn of the century that was doubly mysterious to me because the titles on the bindings had been completely worn off after years of use. My father told me he had acquired these as a student in seminary.

Next to these were volumes by the theologian Paul Tillich (his *Complete History of Christian Thought* and the *Systematic Theology*) and almost a dozen volumes by the visionary Catholic theologian Pierre Teilhard de Chardin, who died about the time I was born. My father, I knew, had written a paper on Teilhard while at seminary — and I especially admired two books by him: *The Phenomenon of Man* and *The Divine Milieu* (both of these were handsome paper editions by Harper Torchbooks which I read, proudly, when I was thirteen).

I now believe as an article of faith that my curious, lifelong obsession with high thought had its origin in these works I venerated — simply in their ambitiously inclusive titles and their muscular physical presence, since it would be years before I was to actually be in any position intellectually to read most of them. What I had absorbed, I think, was something of my father and mother's almost bumpkin Midwestern belief in education, education as the root of morals, of advancement, of anything that is good in life — overcoming even the class structures which otherwise straitjacket societies from top to bottom. Perhaps it went even further: perhaps love and greatness were bound up in me from my earliest years because I loved my father and I thought he was a great man. Indeed, I felt this with all the fierce, abiding conviction of a good son. My father's epic quest for radical meaning — the very meaning which he thought abandoned him in the end — became my own quest. I was his own kind of Telemachus, and I think he always knew this. As for the books, I knew only that they contained answers to any question that a prematurely sad man — or a prematurely sad boy — could possibly pose.

* * *

Christmas 1994 found me in Bellingham, Washington, the city my father died in on April 27 of that year. I had left my wife at the height of her pregnancy — amid some criticism from her family — in order to travel north to Bellingham to assemble and pack my father's library. In the end I shipped home twenty-four boxes of books at a prodigious but necessary cost. In a certain sense, however, I had arrived too late. My father's pessimism — potent, I am convinced, for the five years preceding his death — had done its work. What remained of the huge personal library he and I had built over the years was still impressive, but it was only a semblance of the original.

As near as I have been able to reconstruct, my father had thoughtlessly purged the book collection on two separate occasions: once, some years after moving to Seattle, when a book sale was occurring at the Shoreline Public Library, and he was president of its Friends organization (much of what disappeared then were paperbacks, but none were insignificant). This first *auto-da-fé* erased perhaps a third of the titles in the collection. Another precious moiety of the library disappeared just a year before my father's death, when my parents, for medical reasons, moved to Bellingham to be near my doctor brothers. Prior to leaving Seattle my parents had held a yard sale. The books which finally remained after these subtractions now line the walls in my own study and shall remain there, carving out a *temenos* of their own, transported and reassembled at the other edge of America, where I live, in Laredo, Texas.

* * *

Older, but not old; graying, but not gray — I am a semblance too. Is it true, Father, that there is no salvation? Is that the lesson which you meant by your life — the stern, manly lesson you were trying so hard to teach me at your bedside? Is that why you marred your own creation, which stood in divine analogy to God's? What remains of our library is still prodigious and I value it. Others do too. Perhaps the perfection which our library once achieved, in its tremendous interrelatedness, was illusory or a vanity or merely a childhood dream. Perhaps few books indeed are needed to elucidate the throb of the human heart, and its fade.

You once told me that it is an article of the church that a priest or pastor need not be perfect in himself to deliver the sacraments. Your imperfections, and the deaths and farewells you endured in your life, did sit too heavily on your gentle countenance, I fear. This is what I am trying to tell you, in my own belatedness, amidst the great innerfinishedness of our time.

"In our library you can look up any fact, find any quotation, pursue any inquiry," my father once boasted to me proudly, in better days. He truly believed this, and now I do too. I believe this in spite of all the subtractions of time, chance and calamity — all the inevitable surrenders of life. Our library is poorer now without the three-volume *Encyclopedia of Animals*, Toynbee's great *Study of History*, and the mysterious black biblical encyclopedia that I cannot replace because I never knew its name. We are poorer without Alan Paton's *Too Late the Phalarope* (which is about good fathers and good sons), or our original blue and gold edition of *Wind in the Willows*. *The Frontiers of Astronomy* has vanished, in its beautiful green and black cover — but the *Interpreter's Bible* remains; as does our collection of Paul Tillich, Pierre Teilhard de Chardin, Nikos Kazantzakis and Jacob Bronowski; each a splendid contribution. What remains, my father, is a closed garden which my daughters shall play in: the darling gray-eyed granddaughters you always wanted but did not live to see, and whose life you and your good works shall dignify, in the endless ramifications of print.

"I have never doubted the truth of signs, Adso," the great William

118

of Baskerville tells his young apprentice in Umberto Eco's book *The Name of the Rose*, which began this meditation. "What I did not understand was the relation among signs." Such a lesson explains the futility of all human knowing, the vanity of human wishes and our mysterious obligation to yet know as much as we can.

The Library in Context

A SELECTED, ANNOTATED BIBLIOGRAPHY

Baker, Nicholson, "Discards." *The New Yorker,* April 4, 1994, pp. 64–86.

Never properly or honorably engaged by the profession, this seminal article in the annals of librarianship begins with a discussion of the needless destruction of card catalogs as historical artifacts and goes on to examine why and how this could have occurred. Along the way, Baker, who is an award-winning writer, explores the nature of the new librarianship as revealed by the online catalogs meant to replace the card catalog, and their frequent ineffectiveness, especially for subject searching. Baker, by the way, acknowledges that, especially for the huge research libraries, the card catalog was doomed by the necessity to process and make available records for the glut of books being published during the 1970s and 1980s. What he laments is the fact that the old card catalogs were simply pulped and turned into ignominious refuse. These catalogs he saw as priceless historical treasures, not only of librarianship, but of our common culture. Particularly, they may have been useful to future scholars in ways we cannot know at present. One theme of this book has been the *frenzy* which has accompanied the giddy plunge of librarians into the information void. For all the talk about service we comfort our excesses with, we have in fact done an extremely poor job of listening to a dedicated core of users. Or as a teacher here at our school put it to me recently, "there's actually worse access now."

_____. "The Author vs. the Library." *The New Yorker,* October 14, 1996, pp. 50–62.

Baker's second *New Yorker* installment may be a more embarrassing indictment even than "Discards" about the perverse lengths library administrators will go to conceal their intentions from a discerning public. The feature, replete with details about a lawsuit Baker filed against the San Francisco Public Library, recounts the author's slow uncovering of the wanton destruction of hundreds of thousands of books at San Francisco Public's Main Library during the move to the new city library, which, through poor planning, did not have the space to accommodate them. What occurred was not an orderly "weeding" process. It was a kind of mindless bibliographic genocide, and it cost Library Director Kenneth Dowlin his job once Baker made the facts known to the media. Baker's article also explores the meaning of the new San Francisco Public Library as a symbol of the library of the future: pride of place for computers, inadequate space for books, always beribboned with bone-head promises of (high-priced) infinite "access." It should be apparent from this book's final chapter that I do not see a choice between some version of the old library and the new, or even some murky transitional embodiment. I insist that shortly there will not be any libraries at all.

Bloom, Harold. *The Western Canon: The Books and School of the Ages.* New York: Harcourt Brace, 1994.

A singular assertion of the grandeur and peerlessness of the Canon of great books, even as it is coming under attack in literary studies from Deconstruction, multiculturalism and feminist studies. Bloom, like so many of the authors cited here, writes in an elegiac mode. Why is this? Why are some of our best thinkers united in the belief (which I have only reflected) that some essence has vanished or is vanishing from our society, that it cannot be retrieved because its loss is not even being perceived by the culture at large? Bloom's identification of the heart of the critical enterprise as nothing more complex or contrived than a single person reading a book and coming into an encounter with greatness is, of course, exactly what the Integrated Humanities Program also taught.

Bronowski, Jacob. *Science and Human Values.* New York: Harper Torchbooks, 1965.

Bronowski, like Mortimer Adler, was both a popularizer and a beleaguered optimist and has, therefore, been dismissed by the academy on both counts. This book remains one of the greatest unregarded philosophical treatises of our time, lauding not only the theory and practice of science, but attempting to "safeguard" its achievements within a democratic framework. Bronowski enshrines tolerance, honesty, creativity and discipline as the core values of both science and culture, ideas he also explored in his more well known work for the BBC — the 13-part television series, *The Ascent of Man* (1973).

Cassidy, John, "The Return of Karl Marx." *The New Yorker,* October 20/27, 1997, pp. 248–259.

A trenchant and stimulating discussion of Marx's proof, in *Capital,* of the inevitable tendency of unregulated capitalism to destroy every human value in its path in order to make profits. Such tendencies are currently observable throughout American society, perhaps most overtly in the cynical media conglomerates who prey on our youth.

Crawford, Walt, and Michael Gorman. *Future Libraries: Dreams, Madness and Reality.* Chicago: American Library Association, 1995.

A well-intentioned, well-researched, but somehow dissatisfying, non-visionary book. The authors, both librarians, correctly draw an exact distinction between knowledge and information, but they imagine that the two paradigms (one based on the book, the other on technology) are compatible — a thesis this book explicitly rejects. Technology cannot be wedded to the sacred by any imaginable means, and will always deconstruct it. Thus, in its concluding pages, when Crawford and Gorman laud the dictum "edifice *and* interface" as being part of the library of the future, they fail to grasp that interface has already *eroded* edifice, and will continue to do so, until there is nothing left. Indeed interface will eventually *annihilate* edifice. These are unpleasant realities, of course, but the central thesis of this book is that the library is finished, both inwardly (i.e., ethically) and in physical terms, and that this has been guaranteed by the confluence of professional, cultural and technological events. It is why this book has offered no solutions. Any "solution" offered would be merely the evidence of a repression in knowing.

D'Souza, Dinesh. *Illiberal Education: the Politics of Race and Sex on Campus.* New York: The Free Press, 1991.

D'Souza joins a host of recent social critics who both document and decry a decline in the quality of liberal education in America. In a remarkably comprehensive article spanning educational history, current events, and recent developments in the academy (including multiculturalism and, especially, Deconstruction) D'Souza develops a thesis which I have also cited here in my extended discussion of the Integrated Humanities Program: namely, that modern universities, immersed in a variety of theoretical relativisms and increasingly ensnared by the contending political vagaries of its faculties, have abandoned teaching the humanities *as* the humanities.

Edmundsen, Mark. "On the Uses of a Liberal Education: As Lite Entertainment for Bored College Students." *Harper's,* September, 1997, Vol. 295, No. 1768, pp. 39–49.

This article also chronicles an erosion in liberal arts education in the United States, and especially an erosion in student attitudes and scholastic application due to coddling by college administrators, parents and professors. Edmundsen also cites the immersion of our youth in a media morass that distracts their best efforts in a cynical effort to ensure greater profits by inciting in them an unprecedented appetite for goods they neither need nor benefit from.

Eliot, T.S. *The Complete Poems and Plays, 1909–1950.* New York: Harcourt, Brace & World, Inc., 1971.

The concept of "inner-finishedness" which lies at the heart of the *historical* dimension of this book (and derived from Spengler) finds a still more compelling *poetic* echo in the works of Eliot, who dealt so frequently with the concept of the evacuation of meaning in the modern world. Hence, from *Choruses from the Rock,* the much cited line: "Where is the wisdom we have lost in knowledge? Where is the knowledge we have lost in information?" The implications of this single line for postmodern libraries are impossible to overstate.

Himmelfarb, Gertrude. "Revolution in the Library." *The American Scholar,* Spring 1997, Vol. 66, pp. 197–204.

It will seem almost incredible to readers that I did not "lift" the ideas, even the specific terms, of Dr. Himmelfarb's essay to form the unacknowledged basis of this book. But considering Ms. Himmelfarb's prodigious scholarly reputation, I am a little pleased to note that I did not discover this essay until after the text of the present book was complete and in production. Her understanding of the relationship between the humanities and libraries, her useful-to-a-point stance on technology, and cautionary remarks on technology's power to disintegrate knowledge exactly parallel my own. More remarkable still, she has also cited postmodernism as a species of relativism which is hardly unique to our time. I would humbly venture only one criticism of Professor Himmelfarb's paper: she actually seems to believe that the deleterious effects of technology, even in young minds, can be restrained and that traditional values can, admittedly by great effort, be made to co-exist with "technological" values. Only one so venerably educated already — that is, one fully able to subdue technology with wisdom — could make this almost endearing mistake.

Kaplan, Robert D. "Was Democracy Just a Moment?" *Atlantic,* December, 1997, pp. 55–80.

An incisive anatomy of the perils facing democracy by one of the most learned and insightful social critics now writing. He posits the potential Achilles Heel of democratic systems in the gradual evolution of an oligarchy which subverts the democratic process by slow degrees, compromises all attempts at government regulation and contrives to feed the masses the bread and circuses they always crave. Such a populace, increasingly diverted by entertainments, as in ancient Rome, increasingly sub-educated, sets the stage for ensuing fascism once the economic excesses of the oligarchs have produced catastrophe. This vision of course matches up with the "inner-finishedness" theme of this book — a vision frankly bleak because it deliberately refuses to offer the comfort of "solutions."

Quinn, Dennis B., Ed. *The Integration of Knowledge.* The Integrated Humanities Program, The University of Kansas. Lawrence, Kans., 1979.

This little book outlines the aims and intentions of the professors of the Integrated Humanities Program most effectively, with a contribution by Mortimer Adler entitled "Everybody's Business" (the outline of a speech given at the University of Kansas on March 23, 1978). Dr. Quinn speaks of the necessity of nurturing wonder as the motivating force of all desires to know; Dr. Senior connects the teacher to the student in friendship, which he sees as a species of love; and Frank Nelick, writing from a sound poetic base, laments the decline in liberal arts education. He joins Adler in believing that the restoration of a liberal education based on the great books — unpoliticized and as personal encounters with timeless values — is hopeless. If this bibliography proves anything, it is that, from any number of perspectives, both inside and outside of academe, our culture is ticking dangerously off course; *and that I have merely used libraries — as the greatest extant symbols of wisdom — to underscore this.*

Shorris, Earl. "On the Uses of a Liberal Education: As a Weapon in the Hands of the Restless Poor." *Harper's,* September, 1997, Vol. 295, pp. 50–59.

A moving, quixotic account (a companion piece to 'Edmundsen,' above) of the author's attempt to enfranchise a group of disadvantaged, inner-city minority students into the American Dream by having them read the Great Books and apply their political insights to their own lives. Shorris meets with limited success, but manages to persuade at least some of his students of the value of the enterprise — raising their level of awareness of *how* a controlling culture has cleverly constrained them, and the means by which they can still declare self-hood. This "experiment" is the closest approach I know of to Mortimer Adler's vision of marrying the Great Books, with their aristocratic sensibilities and insight, to the politically and economically disadvantaged.

Sokal, Alan D. "Transgressing the Boundaries: Toward a Transformative Hermeneutics of Quantum Gravity." *Social Text 46/47,* Vol. 14, Nos. 1 and 2, Spring/Summer, 1996.

This howler of an article is actually a fatuous attack on Deconstruction —

aimed right at its heart. Sokal, a recognized physicist at New York University, decided to hoax the journal *Social Text*, the leading light in the field of postmodernism, by submitting his peer-reviewed paper to be published in an issue devoted to the relationship between the sciences and the humanities. Sokal, outrageously, then turned around and revealed the hoax in an article published in the May/June issue of *Lingua Franca*, a journal dedicated to academic debate. The hoax received national attention, making the folks at Duke University, where *Social Text* is published, look like absolute idiots. Among many deliberately unsubstantiated claims which Sokal made, the ludicrousness of which any physics major could have caught, was the contention that the outside world may be socially constructed, i.e., that there *is* no external world. Some deconstructionists have seriously suggested this. In the *Lingua Franca* article, Sokal invites anyone who believes that the laws of physics are socially constructed to step out of his apartment window (he lives on the 21st floor).

Steiner, George. *No Passion Spent: Essays 1978–1995.* [Introduction.] New Haven, Conn.: Yale University Press, 1996.

This lucid introduction to a work about books, reading and translation — rendered with the imperial beauty of Steiner's best prose — highlights both the developments within literary criticism in our time and the advent of high information technology, which he cites as more far reaching even than Gutenberg. He also provides a litany of woes (though he does not cite them as such) of postmodern societies, including, as he says, "the systematic suppression of silence in technological consumer cultures." One hardly needs a specific list to document the general deliquescence of our time: to anyone who can feel, think, read, know, or love it is all too apparent.

Tisdale, Sally. "Silence, Please: the Public Library as Entertainment Center." *Harper's*, March 1997. Vol. 294, pp. 65–68+.

This article chronicles a perceptive user's thoughts about the postmodern library, in a reasoned account with reasoned concerns. It opens with a visit to her library in Portland, Oregon, which turns into a nightmare. Tisdale has entered into an Alice's Restaurant of infotainment where you can have everything — including Alice. The librarian on duty isn't even able to explain the classification system to her. Nor does a visit to one of the major library association conferences bolster her spirits about where we're headed. Tisdale believes, as I do, that the library as a distinctive institution may be vanishing; and she, like Baker, is baffled that the field should choose to substitute respectable, time-honored values — vested in reading — for the tyranny of technology we are permitting to engulf us. The library of her youth she fondly remembers as "the only sacred space I knew."

One recurrent theme of this book, obviously, is the efficacy of lifelong reading. Every statement I have made slamming technology would be entirely moot if we were a culture of reading, or if I could be persuaded that information technology promoted it to the general good. If technology and the libraries it has spawned promoted reading, why would our best user-readers have become, for the first time, our most severe critics?

Wisner, William H. "Back Toward People: A Symposium" [lead article]. *Journal of Academic Librarianship,* July, 1994, pp. 131–133.

A declaration on behalf of traditional values and the reassertion of the human, deliberately provocative and overstated, and designed to spark debate within the profession. I assumed at the time that *JAL* was actually an important journal in the field, but concluded otherwise when I received a whoppin' two responses to my inflammatory statements (both favorable). Perhaps one must simply say that I now believe the profession to be hermetically sealed off from reality, the mere puppet of big business, oblivious to the human, or the implications of its acts, and that perhaps this "inflammatory" essay was not nearly inflammatory enough.

_____. "Whither the Postmodern Library? Confessions of a Doubter." *The Unabashed Librarian,* No. 100, p. 13–14.

This second attempt to signal to the profession its growing dehumanization and spiritual drift was deliberately throttled down to a *non*-provocative mode. Like the *JAL* piece, however, it elicited no response except that of the publisher of the present work.

Index